海岛之光

大榭遗址出土文物精品图录

The Dawn of the Island

The Essential Collection of Archaeological Artefacts at Daxie Site

宁波市文化遗产管理研究院
宁波大榭开发区社会发展保障局
北仑区文物保护管理所 编著

宁波出版社
NINGBO PUBLISHING HOUSE

编撰委员会

主　　任	王　程
副 主 任	韩小寅　黄金国　王结华（执行）
主　　编	王结华
执行主编	雷　少
副 主 编	张华琴　梅术文
编　　委	（以姓氏笔画为序）
	冯　毅　毕显忠　陈兴昌　陈水明
撰　　稿	王结华　雷　少　毕显忠　张华琴
摄　　影	胡冬青　刘　翀
修　　复	史吾平　姚宏均　李养科　郭宗录　王伟国　郑卫国
翻　　译	周昳恒　洪　欣

COMPILATION COMMITTEE

Director: Wang Cheng
Deputy Directors: Han Xiaoyin, Huang Jinguo, Wang Jiehua (Executive)

Chief Editor: Wang Jiehua
Executive Editor: Lei Shao
Associate Editors: Zhang Huaqin, Mei Shuwen
Editorial Board Members: (In the order of the stroke number)
Feng Yi, Bi Xianzhong, Chen Xingchang, Chen Shuiming

Content: Wang Jiehua, Lei Shao, Bi Xianzhong, Zhang Huaqin
Photographers: Hu Dongqing, Liu Chong
Artefacts Restoration: Shi Wuping, Yao Hongjun, Li Yangke, Guo Zonglu, Wang Weiguo, Zheng Weiguo
Translators: Zhou Yiheng, Hong Xin

目 录

001	概　述
025	篇章一　越海而来，文明肇始
	——大榭遗址出土史前时期遗物
028	大榭遗址一期遗存出土遗物
090	大榭遗址二期遗存出土遗物
115	篇章二　向海而生，拓岛有成
	——大榭遗址出土东周时期遗物
129	篇章三　依海而兴，丝路存迹
	——大榭遗址出土宋元时期遗物
176	考古大事记
181	后　记

CONTENTS

001 *Introduction*

025 *Chapter 1 Civilization Begins*
　　　—— Artefacts Excavated at Daxie Site in the Prehistoric Period

028 　The Artefacts Unearthed from Daxie Site Phase 1

090 　The Artefacts Unearthed from Daxie Site Phase 2

115 *Chapter 2 Island Exploitation*
　　　—— Artefacts Excavated at Daxie Site in the Eastern Zhou Dynasty

129 *Chapter 3 Maritime Silk Road Remains*
　　　—— Artefacts Excavated at Daxie Site in Song Dynasty and Yuan Dynasty

176 *Chronicles*

181 *Afterword*

概　述

5000年前，这里开始有了人类劳作的身影；5000年来，这里的文明之火绵延不绝；5000年后的今天，这里已经成为开放的前沿和投资的热土。这就是大榭，一座丰饶而神奇的海岛。

屹立于宁波之东、东海之中的大榭岛，犹如一颗璀璨的海上明珠，镶嵌在舟山群岛与大陆岸线之间。因古时这里树茂林密，远眺仿似浮于茫茫海上的亭台楼阁，故名"大榭"。

岛屿之上，天台山脉东延入海的诸多余脉蜿蜒绵亘、交相错杂，历经千万年的演变，形成了独特的山、岭、岙景观，并将之大体分割成为北岙平原、榭西低地和东、南山地等不同地貌。

环境考古研究表明，距今约9000年前，大榭已经脱离岸陆成为海岛，岛北"U"形平原也逐渐从海湾向潮滩演变；考古发掘成果表明，距今约5000年前，来自宁绍地区的先民开始将目光投向隔海相望的大榭岛，陆续来到榭北盆地涂毛洞山南麓定居，日积月累，最终形成了今天的大榭遗址，曾经僻处一隅、渺无人烟的海岛自此拉开了开发的历史序幕。

1980年9月，当地村民在涂毛洞山下烧窑取土时，曾挖出石锛、石镞等新石器时代磨制石器并上交国家，因为时光流逝而一度深埋地下、不为人知的大榭遗址开始受到关注。

2008年6月，经宁波市第三次全国文物普查，正式确认了遗址的存在，但当时并未命名为大榭遗址，而是根据遗址附近曾有的一座民间小道观——东岳宫，将之定名为"东岳宫遗址"。

2010年10月，"东岳宫遗址"入选"宁波市第三次全国文物普查百大新发现"，并向社会予以公布。

The Dawn of the Island | 海岛之光
大榭遗址出土文物精品图录

大榭遗址地理位置（底图为美国锁眼卫片 1970 年 12 月 6 日影像）
The Location of Daxie Site (The Picture was the US Key Hole Satellite Image taken from 6th of December, 1970)

Introduction 概 述

2015年4月至5月，为配合大榭开发区经济建设，宁波市文物考古研究所（现宁波市文化遗产管理研究院，下同）组织专业人员对大榭遗址进行了多次地面踏查和随机勘探，初步了解了大榭遗址的分布范围和保存状况。

2015年9月至12月，在相关部门的支持配合下，宁波市文物考古研究所主持对大榭遗址开展了先期考古勘探和局部解剖，勘探面积约30000平方米，解剖面积24平方米，出土一批新石器时代的陶、石器文物，并划定了遗址的埋藏区域，明确了遗址的时代跨度和文化内涵，大榭遗址开始渐露真容。

2015年12月17日，因原来的定名容易引发歧义，根据专家论证意见，将"东岳宫遗址"正式改名为"大榭遗址"。

2016年4月至12月、2017年3月至12月，在与宁波大榭开发区管理委员会商定好保护范围的前提下，为支持地方经济建设，经浙江省文物局和国家文物局批准，宁波市文物考古研究所联合全国诸多考古单位和相关科研机构，全方位合作，多学科介入，对总占地约20000平方米的大榭遗址实施了面积达7000平方米的Ⅰ、Ⅱ两期考古发掘并取得重要收获。

经过持续多年科学、严谨、细致、认真的考古调查、勘探、试掘和发掘，大榭遗址先民跌宕起伏、波澜壮阔的生活图景最终得到了相对完整的呈现，大榭这座拥有近5000年悠久历史和深厚文明积淀的海岛也因此散发出炫彩夺目的光芒。

历年考古与研究情况表明，大榭遗址的文化堆积厚约1—2.8米，可分为四大层，时代由早至晚分别为史前、东周和宋元时期。其中，史前时期包括遗址一、二期遗存，时代分别大致相当于良渚文化[①]和钱山漾文化[②]时期，为大榭遗址

---

① 良渚文化因首先发现于浙江省杭州市余杭区良渚镇的古遗址而得名，主要分布在环太湖地区，南达宁绍地区和金衢盆地，北至江苏的长江沿岸地区。据碳十四测年，良渚文化年代距今5300—4300年。它代表了这一地区新石器时代文化发展的最高水平，在长江下游文明化进程中扮演着举足轻重的角色。2019年7月6日，良渚古城遗址被列入世界文化遗产名录。

② 钱山漾文化因首先发现于浙江省湖州市八里店镇钱山漾东南岸的古遗址而得名，主要分布在环太湖地区，南达宁绍地区。据碳十四测年，钱山漾文化年代距今4300—4100年。它开启了环太湖地区新石器时代文化崭新的发展模式，是长江下游地区加快融入以中原为核心的中华文明发展进程的重要见证。

The Dawn of the Island | 海岛之光
大榭遗址出土文物精品图录

大榭遗址Ⅰ、Ⅱ期发掘探方航拍合成照
The Mosaic Photo of the First and Second Excavations of Daxie Site

Introduction
概　述

大樹遺址典型地層堆積剖面示例

The Typical Sections of Stratigraphy of Daxie Site

的主体遗存。

大榭遗址一期遗存以第⑤层堆积为代表。遗迹主要发现有墓葬、灶坑、灰坑、灰沟、烧结面、木桩等。遗物主要出土有大量的陶、石器，还有少量骨、木、竹编器，以及较多陆地、海洋动物骨骼和植物果核。陶器群面貌可分两种：一种以夹砂灰褐陶和泥质黑皮陶为主，器型见有鼎、豆、壶、盘等，具有比较典型的良渚文化特征；另一种则以夹砂红褐陶和粗泥红陶为主，器型见有绳纹釜、小口圈足罐、支脚等，在良渚文化中基本未见，具有鲜明的自身特色。石器见有斧、锛、凿、刀、镞、纺轮等，其中以有段石锛数量最为丰富，且有不少半成品和改形器。

大榭遗址二期遗存以第④层堆积为代表。遗迹主要发现有盐灶、灰坑、陶片堆、制盐废弃物堆等。遗物主要出土有较多陶器和少量石器，以及陆地、海洋动物骨骼。陶器群可分为日用器和制盐器两种：日用陶器较少，多为夹砂红褐陶和泥质灰陶，可辨器型见有鼎、豆、罐、盆、盘等，其既有比较典型的钱山漾文化特征，又有新的文化因素。制盐陶器数量较多，其中：陶缸均为夹砂质地，大口、下腹斜收、圜底；陶盆则有夹植物和贝壳碎屑两种，均为大敞口、浅斜腹、大平底，器胎较厚，火候低。经对盐灶附近和制盐废弃物堆中采集的炭屑样品进行碳十四测年，可知其年代约在公元前 2400—2100 年间。石器出土数量较少，可辨器型见有斧、锛、镞、刀等。玉器仅发现 1 件锥形器。

大榭遗址东周时期文化遗存以第③层堆积为代表。遗迹仅发现有少量灰坑和灰沟。遗物同样出土较少，主要见有夹砂陶鼎、印纹硬陶罐、印纹硬陶坛、原始瓷钵等。

大榭遗址宋元时期文化遗存以第②层堆积为代表。遗迹仅发现有少量灰坑和路面。出土遗物中有大量来自浙江、福建和江西等南方地区不同窑口的瓷器，以及砖、瓦等各类建筑构件。

大榭遗址系在浙东海岛之上首次进行大规模科学发掘的史前文化遗址。两期发掘不仅发现了数量可观的遗迹遗物，更重要的是在其二期遗存中发现了相当于钱山漾文化时期、距今已有 4000 多年悠久历史的海盐业遗存。这可以说是大榭遗址发掘最为主要的收获，也是大榭遗址本身最为突出的价值。

Introduction
概　述

大榭遗址一期遗存土台局部及边坡的废弃物堆积
A Part of an Earth Platform and the Waste Deposite in Its Edge Slope of Daxie Site Phase 1

The Dawn of the Island | 海岛之光
大榭遗址出土文物精品图录

大榭遗址一期储藏坑 H25 及出土遗物
The Storage Pit H25 and Its Unearthed Artefacts of Daxie Site Phase 1

大榭遗址二期土台 I 制盐生产区平面航拍
The Aerial Photo of Salt Manufacture Area of Earth Platform I of Daxie Site Phase 2

Introduction
概　述

当然，大榭遗址的价值并不止于此。2016、2017两年度"浙江考古重要发现"和2016—2017年度全国"田野考古奖"二等奖的获评，以及2017年度"全国十大考古新发现"的入围，已经充分说明了这一点。经2015年12月17日、2016年9月27日、2017年11月10日、2018年3月10日四轮专家论证和持续不断的科学研究，我们可以将其价值简要概括为以下五个方面：

第一，在大榭遗址二期遗存中首次发现了中国沿海地区制造海盐的最早证据。考古过程中不仅揭示出布局较清晰、结构较完整的制盐遗迹，还伴出有种类较丰富、要素较齐全的制盐遗物。这些遗迹遗物与英、德、法等国的盐业遗存非常相似，是中国沿海地区目前发现的制作海盐的最早遗存。其发现与发掘，为探索中国海盐手工业的起源和发展，以及浙东沿海地区的交通、贸易和社会复杂化等重要课题提供了实证，奠定了基础。

第二，大榭遗址一、二期遗存既分别有着比较典型的良渚文化和钱山漾文化因素，又都有新的文化因子注入，展现出新颖的文化特征和鲜明的自身特色。这为构建浙东沿海地区的史前文化序列、完善史前文化谱系提供了新的素材和新的视角。

第三，大榭遗址位居今天的宁绍平原和舟山群岛之间，地理位置独特，"跳板"作用明显，因而对于深入探讨史前时期海陆之间的环境变迁、人地（人海）关系、文化交流与传播、人群迁徙与交往，以及历史时期的"海上丝绸之路"、海洋开发战略及其历史进程，无疑都有着重要的借鉴和参考价值。

第四，大榭遗址的发现，将大榭岛上人类活动和开发建设的历史由原来认知的距今1400年推到了距今5000年左右。这对提升大榭岛的知名度，促进大榭乃至宁波、浙东，甚至整个中国东南沿海地区的理性、有序开发意义非同一般。

第五，在各个层面特别是大榭开发区管委会的支持下，拟建设工程的避让与遗址未发掘区域的填埋保护，以及"海岛之光——大榭遗址考古成果展"的持续展出，充分体现了地方政府对历史文化遗产的重视，也是切实践行国家关于"让历史说话""让文化说话""让文物活起来"等文物保护精神的生动案例。

此外，大榭遗址考古过程中的方法创新和技术探索，譬如环境考古研究、盐业检测分析、盐业实验考古、石器微痕研究和精确测绘、航拍、全程录像、三维建

The Dawn of the Island | 海岛之光
大榭遗址出土文物精品图录

大榭遗址二期盐灶群平面
The Surface of the Salt Manufacture Stoves of Daxie Site Phase 2

大榭遗址二期盐灶群平面
The Surface of the Salt Manufacture Stoves of Daxie Site Phase 2

Introduction
概　述

模、出土人骨鉴定与 DNA 测试等现代科技手段的综合应用，既赢得了业内肯定，也取得了预期效果，同样值得大书特书，唯因篇幅关系，不再一一赘述。

但有一点是无论如何也不能忘却，且必须着重提出的，那就是大榭遗址的成功发掘与保护展示，并非个别单位和某几个人的成就，而是各个层面、社会各界共同努力的结果。借此机会，让我们对以下单位和个人表示最为诚挚的谢忱！

致谢单位（包括但不限于）：

国家文物局；浙江省文物局；宁波市文化广电旅游局；宁波大榭开发区管委会、社会发展保障局、财政局；宁波市自然资源和规划局大榭开发区分局；北仑区文物保护管理所、大榭街道办事处、下厂村村委会；南京大学；中国人民大学；上海市文物保护研究中心；浙江省文物考古研究所；北京大学；复旦大学；山东大学；华东师范大学；洛阳市文物钻探管理办公室（现洛阳市文物勘探中心）……

致谢个人（包括但不限于）：

北京大学教授李水城先生、赵辉先生、张弛先生，副教授崔剑锋先生；中国社会科学院考古研究所所长陈星灿先生，研究员徐光冀先生、赵志军先生，副研究员贾笑冰先生；中国人民大学教授魏坚先生、韩建业先生；中国文物报社李政女士；山东大学教授王青先生、靳桂云女士；山东师范大学教授燕生东先生；上海市文物局副局长褚晓波先生；复旦大学教授高蒙河先生；华东师范大学教授王张华女士；上海市文物保护研究中心副主任翟杨先生；南京大学教授黄建秋先生；江苏省考古研究所副研究员杭涛先生；江西省文物考古研究院研究员周广明先生；广东省文物考古研究所副研究员李岩先生；浙江省文物局副局长郑建华先生，原副局长吴志强先生，文物处处长李新芳女士，综合处处长许常丰先生；浙江省文物考古研究所原所长刘斌先生，副所长方向明先生，研究员孙国平先生、丁品先生、王宁远先生；温州市文物保护考古所副所长梁岩华先生；宁波市文化广电旅游局二级巡视员孟建耀先生、韩小寅先生；原宁波市文化广电新闻出版局副局长舒月明先生，文博处处长徐建成先生、王玉琦先生；宁波博物院院长王力军先生；宁波大榭开发区管委会常务副主任江国梁先生、党工委委员黄金国先生，社会发展保障局原局长杨伟先生、原副局长陈兴昌先生；北仑区文物保护管

The Dawn of the Island | 海岛之光
大榭遗址出土文物精品图录

理所所长冯毅先生、副研究员毕显忠先生……

借此机会,也向曾经具体参与大榭遗址野外考古调查、勘探、发掘与资料整理工作的各位同仁表示衷心感谢!名单如下(包括但不限于):雷少、梅术文、金涛、马彪、陈勤国、余劲、侯鲜婷、朱信通、张灿乐、李胜利、李万正、赵荦、杨天源、张素、朱瑨、刘志佳、刘翀、时萧、张德伟、张政、苗诗钰、姜泽瑞、秦超超、肜海元、张国喜、罗新刚、王发恩、李养科、郭宗录、陈仕光、朱春雨、李铁强、

Introduction
概　述

大榭全景（大榭开发区党工委宣传部供图）
The Full Sight of Daxie (Courtesy of Party Working Committee of Daxie Development Zone)

黄敏、张扬、岑杨、赵碧玉、徐航、张君、孔懿翎、杨君谊、王梦珊、史吾平、冯建科、姚宏均、苗立辉、叶俊士、李雪欣、任冠、刘汉兴、孙锐、郝沁源、汪海伦、王爱梅、李泽浩、谢秉燊、林铃梅、任静依、王晓丹、温馨、周睿麟、李馥禹、赵芃芃、吴景军、寿崇瑞、刘艳坤、仲芹、陈利平、邓瑞英、王海达、马俊……

最后想说的是：

古代的大榭，开发历程跌宕起伏，但从未中断，先民们奔向海洋的脚步一直没有停歇，永远向前的精神从来不曾改变。

今天的大榭，秉承历史遗韵，紧随时代潮流，乘势而行，主动作为，这座神奇而美丽的海岛将打造成为国际一流的临港产业基地、国家能源中转基地和重要的国际贸易基地。

未来的大榭，在国家"一带一路"倡议的推动下，在所有人的共同奋斗下，相信必将描绘出更加精彩的发展蓝图，也必将为保护文化遗产、共建精神家园谱写更加灿烂的永恒篇章。

让我们一起努力！

INTRODUCTION

5000 years ago, the ancestors started to cultivate on the land. During the 5000 years, the civilization of the inhabitants passed on in generations. Nowadays, the place has become a frontier for opening up and a land of investment. It is Daxie, a fertile and magical island.

Located in the east of Ningbo, among the East China Sea, Daxie Island is a pearl of ocean inlaying between the Zhoushan Archipelago and mainland coastline. As the island was heavily forested in the ancient times and looked like a huge construction complex floating on the sea from a distant view, it was named "Daxie" (big pavilion).

The Tiantai Mountains stretched east to the sea. The ranges of the mountains twisted and turned, which reformed the landscape of the island into different landforms such as mountains, hills and valleys. After million years' evolution, it was finally shaped as Bei'ao Plain in the north, Xiexi Lowland in the west, as well as mountainous area in the east and south.

The study of Environmental Archaeology shows that around 9000 years ago, Daxie had separated from the continental plate and became an island. The U-shape Plain in the north of the island also evolved from bay to tidal beach. The archaeological excavation revealed that the ancestors in Ningshao area set their sights on the island across the sea about 5000 years ago and inhabited on the southern foothills of Tumaodong Hill, Xiebei Basin. The long-term settlements of the residents finally formed the site of Daxie. The once isolated and deserted island had begun its journey of exploitation and development.

In September of 1980, local villagers lived on the foothills of Tumaodong Hill discovered Neolithic stone tools such as stone adzes and stone arrowheads while collecting clays for kiln-firing. Later the stone tools were handed over to the government for conservation. As a result, the deep-buried unknown site Daxie started to get attentions.

In June of 2008, the Third National Survey of Cultural Heritage in Ningbo confirmed the existence of the site, but instead of naming it "Daxie", the site was named after a small Taoist temple nearby as "Dongyuegong" Site.

In October of 2010, Dongyuegong Site has been declared as one of the "Top 100 New Discoveries in the Third National Survey of Cultural Heritage in Ningbo" to the public.

From April to May of 2015, in order to support the economic construction of Daxie Development Zone, Ningbo Municipal Institute of Cultural Relics and Archaeology (Ningbo Municipal Institute of Cultural Heritage Management) organized several field investigations and random surveys with expertise. The investigations preliminarily revealed the scope and preservation of the site.

From September to December of 2015, Ningbo Municipal Institute of Cultural Relics and Archaeology conducted an initial survey and a partial trial excavation to Daxie Site under the support and coordination of relevant government departments. The survey covered an area of about 30000 square meters while the trial excavation area was 24 square meters, which unearthed a series of Neolithic potteries and stone artefacts. The archaeological work has determined the location, time span and culture context of the site and revealed the site's true content.

On 17th December of 2015, based on the suggestions from the expert seminar, the site was renamed from "Dongyuegong" to "Daxie" since the original name was a bit ambiguous.

In order to support the local economic development, Ningbo Municipal

Introduction
概　述

Institute of Cultural Relics and Archaeology has fully cooperated with the archaeological organizations and relevant research institutes nationalwide to conduct two multidisciplinary excavations to Daxie Site from April to December of 2016 and March to December of 2017, under the authorizations of the Cultural Heritage Bureau of Zhejiang Province and National Cultural Heritage Administration. Before the excavations, Ningbo Municipal Institute of Cultural Relics and Archaeology had a conversation with Daxie Development Zone Administrative Committee and determined a preservation area of the site. The site in total occupied an area around 20000 square meters while the two excavations reached an area of 7000 square meters, and yielded fruitful achievement.

The long-term scientific, systemic and careful archaeological investigations, surveys, trial excavations and excavations have fully depicted the ups and downs in daily life of ancestors of Daxie site. The Daxie Island with 5000 years history and time-honoured civilization is revitalized.

The archaeological researches over the years demonstrated that the cultural sediment of Daxie Site is around 1-2.8 meters thick and can be divided into four layers dated back to prehistoric period, the Eastern Zhou Dynasty, Song Dynasty and Yuan Dynasty. The prehistoric period can be separated into Phase 1 and Phase 2, which are the time period of Liangzhu Culture[1] and Qianshanyang Culture[2]. The relics of the two phases are the

---

[1] Liangzhu Culture was named after the Liangzhu Town in Yuhang District, Hangzhou, Zhejiang Province where the first ancient site was discovered. These sites were mainly distributed around Taihu Lake rim, Ningshao area and Jinqu Basin to the south, and the bank of Yangtze River in Jiangsu Province to the north. According to Radiocarbon Dating, the date of Liangzhu Culture is around 5300-4300 years ago. It represented the highest level of development of local Neolithic cultures and played an important role in the culture evolution in the downstream of Yangtze River. On 6th July, 2019, the Liangzhu Ancient City Site was officially declared World Cultural Heritage.

[2] Qianshanyang Culture was named after the Qianshanyang Lake in Balidian Town, Huzhou, Zhejiang Province, the southeast bank of which was the original location for the discovery of the ancient site. These sites were mainly distributed around Taihu Lake rim and Ningshao area to the south. According to Radiocarbon Dating, the date of Qianshanyang Culture is around 4300-4100 years ago. It had not only innovated the new development mode for the Neolithic cultures in Taihu Lake rim, but also bore witness to the accelerated process of downstream Yangtze River area fusing into the Chinese civilization which was centred by Central Plains.

main body of Daxie Site.

The relics of Phase 1 of Daxie Site can be represented by the sediment of the Fifth Layer. The features discovered are tombs, stove pits, pits, ditches, sintered surfaces, posts and so on. The artefacts unearthed from the site include pottery wares, stone tools, as well as small amount of bone, wooden and bamboo tools. There are also large amount of terrestrial and marine fauna bones, as well as fruit pits. The potteries discovered from the site can be divided into two categories: the first kind are mainly sandy clay greyish brown pottery and clay pottery with black surface, the types of which include tripod, stem dish, kettle, plate and so on, with classic characteristics of Liangzhu Culture; another kind are mainly sandy clay reddish brown pottery and coarse clay red pottery, with the majority types of cauldron with string decoration, pot with small mouth and ring foot, supporting foot and so on, which are hardly seen in Liangzhu Culture and full of own characters. The stone tools discovered contain axes, adzes, chisels, knives, arrowheads, spinning wheels and so on, within which the stepped adzes were found in most abundant, including semi-finished and modified products.

The relics of Daxie Site Phase 2 can be represented by the sediment of the Fourth Layer. The features found on site include salt manufacture stoves, pits, pottery sediments, salt manufacture wastes and so on. The artefacts unearthed include large amount of pottery wares and small amount of stone tools, as well as some terrestrial and marine fauna bones. Potteries found on site can be divided into daily wares and salt manufacture tools. The daily wares are found in small quantity, with majority of sandy clay reddish brown pottery and clay grey pottery, whose types contain tripod, stem dish, pot, basin, plate and so on. These wares not only bear typical features of Qianshanyang Culture but integrated with new culture elements. On the other hand, salt manufacture wares are superior in numbers, within which the pottery jars were made in sandy clay, with a large mouth, infundibular body and a spherical bottom. In addition, the

Introduction
概 述

pottery basins were made in clay with plants debris as one kind and clay with shell debris as another kind. The basin was shaped in large open mouth, infundibular body with a small angle and a flat bottom, the body of which is relatively thick and fired with a low temperature. After the Radiocarbon Dating of the charcoal samples which collected from the salt manufacture stoves and wastes, the site was dated from 2400-2100 BC. The stone tools are discovered in small amount, with identifiable types as axe, adze, arrowhead, knife, etc. Only one piece of cone-shaped tool made of jade has been discovered.

The relics of Daxie Site in the Eastern Zhou Dynasty can be represented by the sediment of the Third Layer. There are only few pits and ditches discovered on site. The artefacts are also found in small numbers which include sandy clay pottery tripod, stamped hard pottery pot, stamped hard pottery jug, proto-porcelain mortar and so on.

The relics of Daxie Site in Song Dynasty and Yuan Dynasty can be represented by the sediment of the Second Layer. There are only few features such as pits and road surfaces found on site. However, the artefacts unearthed contain large quantity of porcelains from southern provinces such as Zhejiang, Fujian and Jiangxi provinces, as well as construction materials such as bricks and tiles.

Daxie Site is the first prehistoric site scientifically excavated in large scale on the island of east Zhejiang Province. The two excavations not only discovered a substantial number of artefacts and features, but also revealed the remains of sea salt manufacture in the Phase 2 relics which are roughly 4000 years old and the same period with Qianshanyang Culture. This is the major achievement of the excavation of Daxie Site, as well as its biggest importance.

Nevertheless, Daxie Site values more. It has been awarded twice with "The Important Archaeological Discoveries of Zhejiang" in 2016 and 2017, a second prize of "the National Field Archaeology Award" from 2016 to 2017, and nominated for "The National Top Ten Archaeological New Discoveries" in 2017. The honours have fully proved itself. There were four expert seminars which were on 17th December of 2015, 27th September of 2016, 10th November of 2017 and 10th March of 2018 based on the site. Combined with the results of the seminars and continuous scientific studies on the remains, we can now briefly summarize the value of the site into following five aspects.

First, the earliest evidence of salt manufacture in Chinese coastal area has been found in the remains of Daxie Site Phase 2. During the archaeological work, the features of salt manufacture which have a clear layout and complete structure were revealed. In addition, the site unearthed a full range of salt-manufacture artefacts. These relics as the first discovered salt manufacture site in coastal area of China are in great similarity with the salt industry remains in countries such as the UK, Germany and France. Its discoveries and excavations have explored the origin and development of sea-salt manufacture in China, and offered solid evidence for the important thesis such as the transportation, trade and society complex in coastal areas of East Zhejiang Province.

Second, Daxie Site has its unique cultural features and distinct characteristics as it not only involved with classic elements of Liangzhu Culture and Qianshanyang Culture, but also embraces new cultural factors. Therefore the site offers new perspective and new materials for the construction of prehistoric sequence and completion of prehistoric culture genealogy in coastal area of East Zhejiang Province.

Third, Daxie site is located between nowadays Ningshao Plain and Zhoushan Islands. Its unique geographic position makes it a "bridge" between land and sea. Thus the site is an important reference for the research of environmental change of land and sea in prehistoric times, the human-land (human-ocean) relationships, the cultural communication and exchange, migration and communication, the history of "Maritime Silk Road", as well as the marine developing strategies and its history.

Fourth, the discovery of Daxie site has pushed the history of human activities and developments on the Daxie Island from 1400 years ago to 5000 years ago. The archaeological work raises the popularity of the island and has a positive impact on fostering a rational and orderly development plan of Daxie Island. The benefit was shared even to Ningbo, East Zhejiang Province and the whole coastal areas of Southeast China.

Fifth, under the support of all the social sectors, especially the Daxie Development Zone Administrative Committee, the original construction plan has been changed and the unexcavated area of the site has been able to protect *in situ*. Moreover, "The Dawn of the Island—The Exhibition of Archaeological Achievements at Daxie Site" has been continuously displayed in local area. The activities have demonstrated the emphasis on the cultural heritage of the local government, which is also a good case study of the national strategy to revitalize the history, culture and artefacts.

In addition, the new methodologies and technologies have been adopted during the archaeological work of the Daxie Site such as environmental archaeology, salt industry detection, salt industry laboratory, lithic micromark study, precise surveying, aerial photography, whole process video, 3D modelling, physical anthropology and DNA detection, the adoption of which has been recognised and the results are inspiring. However, due to the limitation of the words, the details will not be expatiated in this book.

However, there is one particular point need to be emphasized that the success of the excavation, conservation and display of Daxie Site is not owing to a single institute or several scholars, but the efforts of all sectors of society. We would like to take the opportunity and give our sincere appreciation to the following institutes and personnel.

Acknowledgement to (but not limited to) the organizations:

National Cultural Heritage Administration, the Cultural Heritage Bureau of Zhejiang Province, Ningbo Municipal Bureau of Culture, Radio, Television and Tourism, Ningbo Daxie Development Zone Administrative Committee, Ningbo Daxie Development Zone Social Development and Security Administration, Ningbo Daxie Development Zone Finance Bureau, Ningbo Daxie Development Zone Sub-bureau of Ningbo Bureau of Natural Resources and Planning, Beilun District Cultural Relics Protection and Management Institute, Daxie Sub-district Office, Committee of Xiachang Village, Nanjing University, Renmin University of China, Shanghai Cultural Relics Protection Research Center, Zhejiang Provincial Institute of Cultural Relics and Archaeology, Peking University, Fudan University, Shandong University, East China Normal University, Luoyang Municipal Management Office of Cultural Relics and Survey (Now Luoyang Municipal Center of Cultural Relics and Survey), etc.

Acknowledgement to (but not limited to) the following individuals:

Professor Li Shuicheng, Professor Zhao Hui, Professor Zhang Chi and Vice Professor Cui Jianfeng from Peking University; Curator Mr. Chen Xingcan, Researcher Xu Guangyi, Researcher Zhao Zhijun and Vice Researcher Jia Xiaobing from Institute of Archaeology Chinese Academy of Social Sciences; Professor Wei Jian and Professor Han Jianye from Renmin University of China; Ms. Li Zheng from China Cultural Relics Newspaper; Professor Wang Qing and Professor Jin Guiyun from Shandong University; Professor Yan Shengdong from Shandong Normal University; Deputy Director Mr. Chu Xiaobo from Shanghai Municipal Administration of Culture Heritage; Professor Gao Menghe from Fudan University; Professor Wang Zhanghua from East China Normal University; Vice Director Mr. Zhai Yang from Shanghai Cultural Relics Protection Research Center; Professor Huang

Introduction
概　述

Jianqiu from Nanjing University; Vice Researcher Hang Tao from Jiangsu Provincial Institute of Archaeology; Researcher Zhou Guangming from Jiangxi Provincial Institute of Cultural Relics and Archaeology; Vice Researcher Li Yan from Guangdong Provincial Institute of Cultural Relics and Archaeology; Deputy Director Mr. Zheng Jianhua, Former Deputy Director Mr. Wu Zhiqiang, Director of Cultural Relics Department Ms. Li Xinfang and Director of General Office Mr. Xu Changfeng from the Cultural Heritage Bureau of Zhejiang Province; Previous Director Mr. Liu Bin, Deputy Director Mr. Fang Xiangming, Researcher Sun Guoping, Researcher Ding Pin and Researcher Wang Ningyuan from Zhejiang Provincial Institute of Cultural Relics and Archaeology; Deputy Director Mr. Liang Yanhua from Wenzhou Municipal Institute of Cultural Relics and Archaeology; Secondary Inspector Mr. Meng Jianyao and Inspector Mr. Han Xiaoyin from Ningbo Municipal Bureau of Culture, Radio, Television and Tourism; Deputy Director Mr. Shu Yueming, Director of Cultural Relics and Museum Department Mr. Xu Jiancheng, Mr. Wang Yuqi from Former Culture, Radio, Television, News and Publication Bureau of Ningbo; Curator Mr. Wang Lijun from Ningbo Museum; Executive Deputy Director Mr. Jiang Guoliang, Member of the Party Working Committee Mr. Huang Jinguo from Ningbo Daxie Development Zone Administrative Committee; Former Director Mr. Yang Wei and Former Deputy Director Chen Xingchang from Ningbo Daxie Development Zone Social Development and Security Administration; Director Mr. Feng Yi and Vice Researcher Bi Xianzhong from Beilun District Cultural Relics Protection and Management Institute; etc.

We would like to express our sincere appreciation to (but not limited to) the following members who anticipated in the archaeological field investigations, surveys, excavations and organization of data: Lei Shao, Mei Shuwen, Jin Tao, Ma Biao, Chen Qinguo, Yu Jin, Hou Xianting, Zhu Xintong, Zhang Canle, Li Shengli, Li Wanzheng, Zhao Luo, Yang Tianyuan, Zhang Su, Zhu Jin, Liu Zhijia, Liu Chong, Shi Xiao, Zhang Dewei, Zhang Zheng, Miao Shiyu, Jiang Zerui, Qin Chaochao, Rong Haiyuan, Zhang

Guoxi, Luo Xingang, Wang Faen, Li Yangke, Guo Zonglu, Chen Shiguang, Zhu Chunyu, Li Tieqiang, Huang Min, Zhang Yang, Cen Yang, Zhao Biyu, Xu Hang, Zhang Jun, Kong Yiling, Yang Junyi, Wang Mengshan, Shi Wuping, Feng Jianke, Yao Hongjun, Miao Lihui, Ye Junshi, Li Xuexin, Ren Guan, Liu Hanxing, Sun Rui, Hao Qinyuan, Wang Hailun, Wang Aimei, Li Zehao, Xie Bingshen, Lin Lingmei, Ren Jingyi, Wang Xiaodan, Wen Xin, Zhou Ruilin, Li Fuyu, Zhao Pengpeng, Wu Jingjun, Shou Chongrui, Liu Yankun, Zhong Qin, Chen Liping, Deng Ruiying, Wang Haida, Ma Jun, etc.

Last but not least, the exploration of the ancient Daxie was full of difficulties, however, the ancestors never stopped their steps to explore the ocean and their forward spirit lasts.

The present Daxie inherits its history and catches the current of the time. It is highly motivated to build this magic and beautiful island into an international advanced port-surrounding industrial base, a national energy transfer base and an important international commercial base.

In addition, under the promotion of the Belt and Road Initiative of China, Daxie will have a more splendid blueprint in the future through the efforts of its citizens. It is also believed that the culture heritage protection and spiritual construction in the future Daxie would be more advanced.

Let's work hard together!

篇章一 Chapter 1

越海而来，
文明肇始

——大榭遗址出土史前时期遗物

Civilization Begins

——Artefacts Excavated at Daxie Site in the Prehistoric Period

海岛之光
The Dawn of the Island | 大榭遗址出土文物精品图录

距今约5000年前，先民们陆续越海而来，选择在大榭岛的涂毛洞山脚下定居，以岛为家，耕海牧渔，煮海为盐，点亮了大榭的第一缕文明曙光，掀起了大榭开发建设的第一轮浪潮。

在距今约5000—4400年的大榭遗址一期（相当于良渚文化时期）遗存中，不仅发现了诸多木桩、储藏坑、灶坑、灰坑、烧结面、墓葬等重要遗迹110余处，同时还出土了大量陶器、石器，少量骨器和竹编、木构件等文物400余件，以及丰富的陆地、海洋动物骨骸和较多橡子、南酸枣、葫芦、甜瓜等植物果核。其中磨制精细、形制规整的各式石器，形制多样、造型古朴的各类陶器，以及陶胎中常见的水稻谷壳印痕的发现，表明当时的大榭先民已经熟练掌握了伐木制作、水稻种植、炼泥制陶等技艺，并在静寂的海岛之上描绘出一幅辛勤耕织、渔猎山海、炊烟袅袅的远古生活画卷。

在距今约4400—4100年的大榭遗址二期（相当于钱山漾文化时期）遗存中，发现了迄今为止我国最早的海盐业遗存。这里不仅有大量成组排列、结构清晰的盐灶和少量卤水坑等盐业生产遗迹，还有制盐废弃物堆多处，同时也出土了数量众多且极具特色的陶质盐缸、盐盆和支脚等盐业生产用具，以及较多陶、石器和少量玉器等日常生活用具100余件。当时的大榭先民，就是利用这些简陋的工具，取海作卤、煮卤成盐，开我国海盐生产之先河，为古代海盐业的兴起与发展立下了首创之功。

Chapter 1

篇章一 越海而来，文明肇始

About 5,000 years ago, the ancestors came across the sea and chose to settle at the foot of Tumaodong Mountain in Daxie Island. They took the island as their home, where they invested in fisheries and made salt by distilling the sea water. They lightened the first dawn of civilization on Daxie Island, and set off the first wave of its development and construction.

In the first phase of Daxie Site about 5000-4400 years ago (equivalent to Liangzhu Culture), more than 110 important features have been excavated, such as posts, storage pits, stove pits, ash pits, sintered surfaces, tombs and so on. At the same time, more than 400 artefacts were unearthed which include large numbers of pottery wares, stone tools, a small amount of bone artefacts and bamboo, wooden components, as well as a wealth of terrestrial and marine animal bones, and kernels of acorns, choerospondias axillaris, gourds, melons and so on. All kinds of fine grinding, well-shaped stone tools, variously-shaped but simple-decorated pottery wares, especially the discovery of rice husk marks on pottery body indicate that the ancestors of Daxie Island had mastered the techniques of logging, rice cultivation, and clay firing. They depicted an ancient life picture of cultivating, weaving, fishing and hunting shrouded by smoke spiraling from kitchens on that peaceful and tranquil island.

In the second phase of Daxie Site about 4400-4100 years ago (equivalent to Qianshanyang Culture), the earliest sea salt manufacture remains in China have been found. There are not only a large number of salt production features such as salt manufacture stoves arranged in groups with clear structure and a small number of brine pits, but also plenty of salt making waste deposits have been excavated. In the meantime, a large number of salt production tools such as pottery salt jars, salt basins and stands, as well as more than 100 pieces of daily necessities which include pottery wares, stone tools and a small amount of jade accessories have been unearthed. The ancestors living on Daxie Island used such primitive tools to extract brine from seawater and then boiled the brine into salt, which became the pioneer of China's sea salt industry and made great contributions to its rise and development.

The Dawn of the Island | 海 岛 之 光
大榭遗址出土文物精品图录

大榭遗址一期遗存出土遗物
The Artefacts Unearthed from Daxie Site Phase 1

　　大榭遗址一期遗存出土遗物主要有大量的陶、石器，还有少量骨、木、竹编器，以及较多陆地、海洋动物骨骼和植物果核。陶器群面貌可分两种：一种以夹砂灰褐陶和泥质黑皮陶为主，器型见有鼎、豆、壶、盘等，具有比较典型的良渚文化特征；另一种则以夹砂红褐陶和粗泥红陶为主，器型见有绳纹釜、小口圈足罐、支脚等，在良渚文化中基本未见，具有鲜明的自身特色。石器见有斧、锛、凿、刀、镞、纺轮等，其中以有段石锛数量最为丰富，且有不少半成品和改形器。陆地动物骨骼以鹿类最多，还有猪、狗等。海洋动物骨骼以泥蚶数量最多，其次为鱼类骨骼。植物果核主要有南酸枣、桃、梅、小葫芦、甜瓜属、橡子、松属等。

The artefacts unearthed from Daxie Site Phase 1 include pottery wares, stone tools, as well as small amount of bone, wooden and bamboo tools. There are also large numbers of terrestrial and marine fauna skeletons, as well as fruit pits. The potteries discovered can be divided into two categories: the first kind are mainly sandy clay greyish brown pottery and clay pottery with black surface, the types of which include tripod, stem dish, kettle, plate and so on, with classic characteristics of Liangzhu Culture; another kind are mainly sandy clay reddish brown pottery and coarse clay red pottery, the majority types of which are cauldron with string decoration, pot with small mouth and ring foot, supporting foot and so on. The latter are hardly seen in Liangzhu Culture and full of own characters. The stone tools unearthed contain axes, adzes, chisels, knives, arrowheads, spinning wheels and so on, within which the stone stepped adzes were found in most abundant, including semi-finished and modified products. The animal bones were mainly belong to deer, and few pig and dog bones, while the marine remains were mainly clams, followed by fish bones. The fruit pits discovered were choerospondias axillaris, peaches, plums, gourds, melons, acorns, pine nuts and so on.

Chapter 1

篇章一 越海而来,文明肇始

陶 鼎
Pottery Tripod
高 23.2 厘米　口径 22.8 厘米
H52∶1

| The Dawn of the Island | 海岛之光
大榭遗址出土文物精品图录

陶 鼎
Pottery Tripod
高 29.4 厘米　口径 26 厘米　腹径 27.5 厘米
TG2 ②：1

陶 鼎
Pottery Tripod
高 18.1 厘米　口径 30 厘米
T0906 ⑤ c1：51

Chapter 1
篇章一　越海而来，文明肇始

陶　鼎
Pottery Tripod
高 28.9 厘米　口径 25.2 厘米
T0909 ⑤ c2∶3

The Dawn of the Island | 海 岛 之 光
大榭遗址出土文物精品图录

陶 鼎
Pottery Tripod
高 20.4 厘米　口径 12 厘米
T1005 ⑤ f : 1

Chapter 1
篇章一　越海而来，文明肇始

陶 鼎
Pottery Tripod
高 21.9 厘米　口径 23.5 厘米　腹径 21 厘米
T1007 ⑤ d1：3

033

The Dawn of the Island | 海岛之光
大榭遗址出土文物精品图录

陶 釜
Pottery Cauldron
高 18.8 厘米　口径 22.6 厘米
H50 ①：1

陶 釜
Pottery Cauldron
高 16.7 厘米　口径 14.3 厘米　腹径 26.9 厘米
H52：2

Chapter 1
篇章一 越海而来，文明肇始

陶 釜
Pottery Cauldron
高 11.4 厘米　口径 10.2 厘米　腹径 14.3 厘米
T0907 ⑤ f1 : 8

陶 釜
Pottery Cauldron
高 20.5 厘米　口径 19 厘米
T0907 ⑤ f1 : 9

The Dawn of the Island | 海岛之光
大榭遗址出土文物精品图录

陶 釜
Pottery Cauldron
高 14.7 厘米　口径 12.5 厘米　腹径 18.4 厘米
T1007 ⑤ d1：5

陶单耳釜
Pottery Cauldron with Ear
高 11.5 厘米　口径 9.7—11 厘米　腹径 13.6 厘米
T1108 ⑤ c：2

Chapter 1

篇章一 越海而来，文明肇始

鸟首形陶支脚
Bird Head Shaped Pottery Stand
高 18.3 厘米　底径 10.2 厘米
T0906 ⑤ c1：54

陶支脚
Pottery Stand
高 16.6 厘米　底径 10.2 厘米
T0906 ⑤ c1：60

The Dawn of the Island | 海岛之光
大榭遗址出土文物精品图录

陶 豆
Pottery Stem Dish
高 10.1 厘米　口径 18.6 厘米　底径 12.8 厘米
T0906 ⑤ c1 : 81

陶 豆
Pottery Stem Dish
高 7.5 厘米　口径 19.4 厘米　底径 14 厘米
H28 : 2

Chapter 1
篇章一　越海而来，文明肇始

陶　豆
Pottery Stem Dish
高 7.5 厘米　口径 16.2 厘米　底径 10.6 厘米
T0908 ⑤ e2：1

陶　豆
Pottery Stem Dish
高 9.8 厘米　口径 16.4 厘米　底径 10.6 厘米
T0909 ⑤ c2：4

The Dawn of the Island | 海 岛 之 光
大榭遗址出土文物精品图录

陶 豆
Pottery Stem Dish
高 9.5 厘米　口径 17 厘米　底径 14.2 厘米
T1007 ⑤ c : 5

陶 豆
Pottery Stem Dish
高 14.9 厘米　口径 16.6 厘米　底径 9.4 厘米
T1108 ⑤ c : 5

Chapter 1
篇章一 越海而来,文明肇始

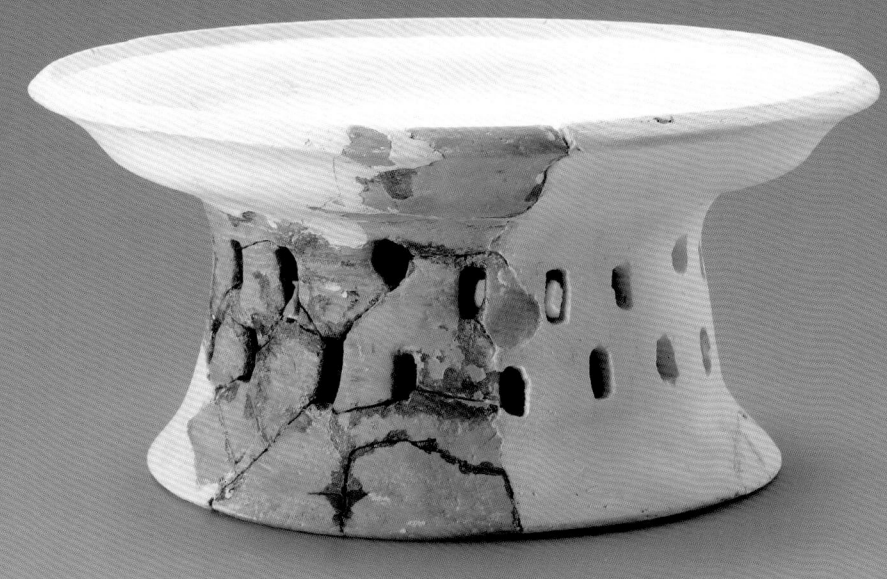

陶 豆
Pottery Stem Dish
高 11.7 厘米　口径 23.6 厘米　底径 18.8 厘米
T1207 ⑤ b：8

The Dawn of the Island | 海 岛 之 光
大榭遗址出土文物精品图录

陶 罐
Pottery Pot
高 31 厘米　口径 19.8 厘米　底径 14.4 厘米
T1008 ⑤ d：1

Chapter 1
篇章一 越海而来,文明肇始

陶 罐
Pottery Pot
高 8.9 厘米 口径 9.6 厘米
T1007 ⑤ d1:4

The Dawn of the Island | 海岛之光
大榭遗址出土文物精品图录

陶双鼻壶
Pottery Bottle with Double Ears
高 11.8 厘米　口径 6.4 厘米　腹径 7.7 厘米
M1：3

陶双鼻壶
Pottery Bottle with Double Ears
高 12.4 厘米　口径 6.4 厘米　腹径 8 厘米
T0809 ⑤ c：1

Chapter 1

篇章一 越海而来，文明肇始

陶双鼻壶
Pottery Bottle with Double Ears
高 12—13.5 厘米　口径 7.8—8.5 厘米　腹径 12.7 厘米
T1008 ⑤ c : 4

045

The Dawn of the Island | 海岛之光
大榭遗址出土文物精品图录

陶三足盘
Pottery Tripod Plate
高 21.2 厘米　口径 19.5 厘米
T0807 ⑤ c2：1

Chapter 1
篇章一 越海而来，文明肇始

陶圈足盘
Pottery Plate with Ring Foot
高 7.8 厘米　口径 20.8 厘米　底径 13.6 厘米
H20∶1

陶圈足盘
Pottery Plate with Ring Foot
高 8.5 厘米　口径 21.4 厘米　底径 17.8 厘米
T0810 ⑤ a∶7

陶圈足盘
Pottery Plate with Ring Foot
高 5.6 厘米　口径 22.8 厘米　底径 16 厘米
T0810 ⑤ c：16

陶圈足盘
Pottery Plate with Ring Foot
高 13.3 厘米　口径 21 厘米　底径 15.8 厘米
T1104 ⑤ b：1

Chapter 1
篇章一 越海而来，文明肇始

陶圈足盘
Pottery Plate with Ring Foot
高 7.3 厘米　口径 19.6 厘米　底径 13.8 厘米
T0907 ⑤ f2：1

陶圈足盘
Pottery Plate with Ring Foot
高 8.1 厘米　口径 20.6 厘米　底径 14.8 厘米
T1205 ⑤ b：5

The Dawn of the Island | 海岛之光
大榭遗址出土文物精品图录

陶带流钵
Pottery Mortar with Spout
高 11.5 厘米　口径 23.8 厘米
T0810 ⑤ c : 4

陶带流钵
Pottery Mortar with Spout
高 12.4 厘米　口径 21—22.6 厘米
T0910 ⑤ a : 3

陶器盖
Pottery Lid
高 4.5 厘米　底径 17.2 厘米
H31 : 1

Chapter 1
篇章一 越海而来，文明肇始

石 斧
Stone Axe
长 13.5 厘米　宽 4.2 厘米　厚 4.4 厘米
T0907 ⑤ e2：1

石 斧
Stone Axe
长 15.25 厘米　宽 4.6 厘米　厚 4.8 厘米
T0908 ⑤ c2：1

051

The Dawn of | 海 岛 之 光
the Island | 大榭遗址出土文物精品图录

有段石锛
Stone Stepped Adze
长 6.9 厘米　宽 3.8 厘米　厚 2.1 厘米
T0807 ⑤ c1：17

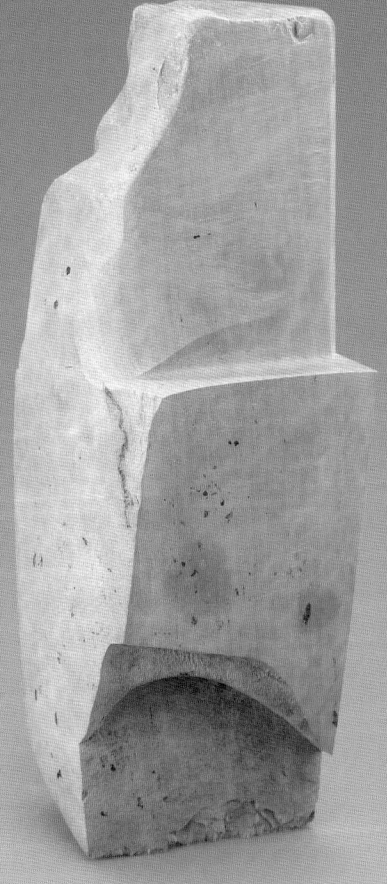

有段石锛
Stone Stepped Adze
长 9 厘米　宽 3 厘米　厚 2.5 厘米
T0709 ⑤ a：3

Chapter 1
篇章一 越海而来，文明肇始

有段石锛
Stone Stepped Adze
长 10.2 厘米　宽 6 厘米　厚 1.4 厘米
T0806 ⑤ c1：1

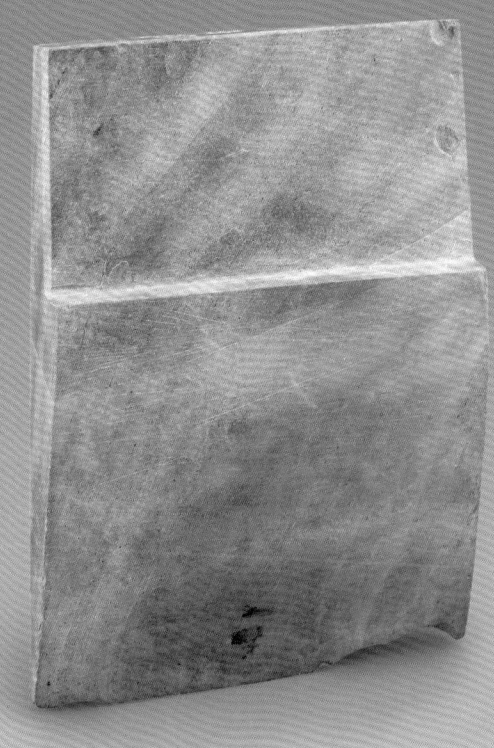

有段石锛
Stone Stepped Adze
长 7.7 厘米　宽 5.8 厘米　厚 1.3 厘米
T0806 ⑤ c1：2

The Dawn of | 海 岛 之 光
the Island | 大榭遗址出土文物精品图录

有段石锛
Stone Stepped Adze
长 7.3 厘米　宽 2.7 厘米　厚 1.2 厘米
T0806 ⑤ c1：4

有段石锛
Stone Stepped Adze
长 9.5 厘米　宽 5.8 厘米　厚 1.4 厘米
T0807 ⑤ c1：10

Chapter 1
篇章一 越海而来，文明肇始

有段石锛
Stone Stepped Adze
长 7 厘米　宽 2.8 厘米　厚 0.7 厘米
T0906 ⑤ c1：21

有段石锛
Stone Stepped Adze
长 11.7 厘米　宽 5.2 厘米　厚 2.7 厘米
T0807 ⑤ f1：4

有段石锛
Stone Stepped Adze
长 5.9 厘米　宽 3.6 厘米　厚 1.1 厘米
T0810 ⑤ a：1

有段石锛
Stone Stepped Adze
长 8.2 厘米　宽 4.7 厘米　厚 2.4 厘米
T0809 ⑤ a2：5

Chapter 1

篇章一 越海而来，文明肇始

有段石锛
Stone Stepped Adze
长 12.2 厘米　宽 5.6 厘米　厚 2.1 厘米
T0807 ⑤ f1：2

有段石锛
Stone Stepped Adze
长 11.8 厘米　宽 3.46 厘米　厚 3.35 厘米
T0807 ⑤ f1：3

The Dawn of the Island | 海岛之光
大榭遗址出土文物精品图录

有段石锛
Stone Stepped Adze
长 13.7 厘米　宽 4.8 厘米　厚 2.4 厘米
T0905 ⑤ b1：1

有段石锛
Stone Stepped Adze
长 12.5 厘米　宽 5.5 厘米　厚 2.2 厘米
T0907 ⑤ e2：3

Chapter 1
篇章一　越海而来，文明肇始

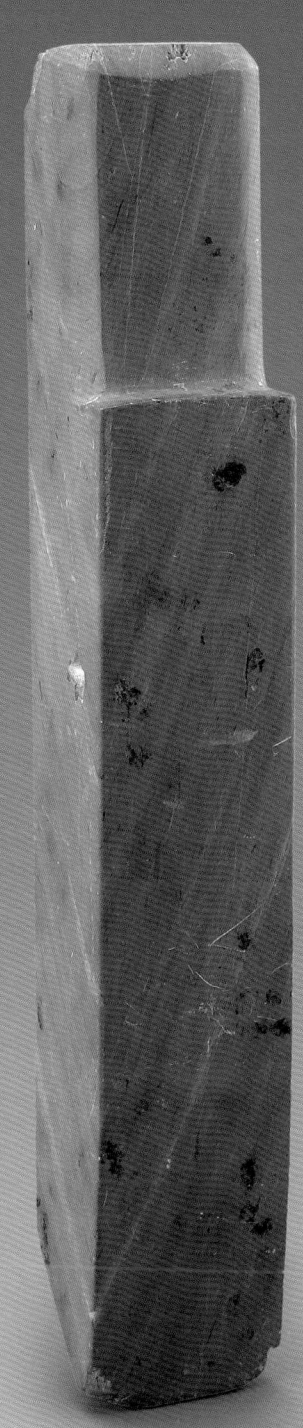

有段石锛
Stone Stepped Adze
长 18.1 厘米　宽 3 厘米　厚 2.9 厘米
T1007 ⑤ c：2

有段石锛
Stone Stepped Adze
长 6.9 厘米　宽 5.3 厘米　厚 1.2 厘米
T1105 ⑤ c: 1

有段石锛
Stone Stepped Adze
长 4.26 厘米　宽 2.34 厘米　厚 7.95 厘米
T1208 ⑤ a: 1

Chapter 1
篇章一 越海而来，文明肇始

有段石锛
Stone Stepped Adze
长 3.5 厘米　宽 2.3 厘米　厚 1.2 厘米
T1208 ⑤ a：8

有段石锛
Stone Stepped Adze
长 4.2 厘米　宽 2.9 厘米　厚 1.3 厘米
T1308 ⑤ a：5

The Dawn of | 海岛之光
the Island | 大榭遗址出土文物精品图录

石 锛
Stone Adze
长 7.8 厘米　宽 5.5 厘米　厚 1.7 厘米
T0806 ⑤ c1：3

石 锛
Stone Adze
长 7.8 厘米　宽 3 厘米　厚 2.2 厘米
T0808 ⑤ a2：6

Chapter 1
篇章一 越海而来，文明肇始

石 锛
Stone Adze
长 4 厘米　宽 2.6 厘米　厚 1 厘米
T0807 ⑤ d2：4

石 锛
Stone Adze
长 10.6 厘米　宽 6 厘米　厚 1.3 厘米
T1208 ⑤ a：6

The Dawn of the Island | 海岛之光
大榭遗址出土文物精品图录

弧刃石锛
Stone Adze with a Curved Blade
长 17.11 厘米 宽 5.82 厘米 厚 5.44 厘米
T0709 ⑤ a: 2

弧刃石锛
Stone Adze with a Curved Blade
长 10.7 厘米 宽 6.1 厘米 厚 2.5 厘米
T0806 ⑤ c1: 6

Chapter 1
篇章一 越海而来，文明肇始

弧刃石锛
Stone Adze with a Curved Blade
长 10.2 厘米　宽 4.3 厘米　厚 2.1 厘米
T0806 ⑤ c2：1

弧刃石锛
Stone Adze with a Curved Blade
长 12.05 厘米　宽 5.75 厘米　厚 2.94 厘米
T0807 ⑤ f1：1

The Dawn of the Island | 海岛之光
大榭遗址出土文物精品图录

石 刀
Stone Knife
长 7.68 厘米　宽 2.75 厘米　厚 0.55 厘米
T0907⑤f1：6

Chapter 1
篇章一 越海而来，文明肇始

双孔石刀
Stone Knife with Double Holes
长 19.7 厘米　宽 9 厘米
T0809 ⑤ a2：6

双孔石刀
Stone Knife with Double Holes
长 14.9—15.9 厘米　宽 7 厘米
M1∶2

Chapter 1

篇章一 越海而来，文明肇始

双孔石刀
Stone Knife with Double Holes
长 13 厘米　宽 8.5 厘米　厚 0.4 厘米
M2 : 1

The Dawn of the Island | 海 岛 之 光
大榭遗址出土文物精品图录

靴形石刀
Boot-shaped Stone Knife
长 9.6 厘米 宽 7.7 厘米 厚 0.71 厘米
T0906 ⑤ c1：19

斜把石刀
Stone Knife with Handle
长 10.8 厘米 宽 5.4 厘米 厚 0.3 厘米
T0906 ⑤ c1：23

Chapter 1
篇章一 越海而来，文明肇始

石 钺
Stone Battleaxe
长 9 厘米　宽 5 厘米　厚 0.8 厘米
T0907 ①：2

石 钺
Stone Battleaxe
长 13.8 厘米　宽 11 厘米　厚 1.2 厘米
T1006 ①：4

071

The Dawn of the Island	海岛之光
	大榭遗址出土文物精品图录

石 镞
Stone Arrowhead
长 5.7 厘米　宽 1.2 厘米　厚 0.4 厘米
T0807 ⑤ c1：1

石 镞
Stone Arrowhead
长 5.3 厘米　宽 2 厘米　厚 0.3 厘米
T0711 ⑤ a：1

Chapter 1
篇章一 越海而来，文明肇始

石 镞
Stone Arrowhead
长 5.7 厘米　宽 1.4 厘米　厚 0.3 厘米
T0807 ⑤ c1: 2

石 镞
Stone Arrowhead
长 8.8 厘米　宽 2 厘米　厚 0.8 厘米
T0809 ⑤ a1: 1

The Dawn of the Island | 海 岛 之 光
大榭遗址出土文物精品图录

石 镞
Stone Arrowhead
长 8.3 厘米　宽 2.2 厘米　厚 0.8 厘米
T0907 ⑤ d1 : 1

石 镞
Stone Arrowhead
长 8 厘米
T0809 ⑤ a1 : 5

Chapter 1
篇章一 越海而来，文明肇始

石 镞
Stone Arrowhead
长 13.31 厘米 宽 2.04 厘米 厚 1.17 厘米
T1007 ⑤ d2：1

石 镞
Stone Arrowhead
长 11.9 厘米 宽 2.4 厘米 厚 1.4 厘米
T0806 ⑤ c1：5

The Dawn of the Island | 海岛之光
大榭遗址出土文物精品图录

石　镞
Stone Arrowhead
长 6.7 厘米　宽 2.3 厘米　厚 0.5 厘米
T0907 ⑤ e2：12

石　镞
Stone Arrowhead
长 7.5 厘米　宽 2 厘米　厚 0.8 厘米
T1008 ⑤ b：1

Chapter 1
篇章一 越海而来，文明肇始

石 镞
Stone Arrowhead
长 9 厘米
T1009 ⑤ b : 2

石 镞
Stone Arrowhead
长 7.9 厘米　宽 2 厘米　厚 0.8 厘米
T1407 ⑤ a : 1

石犁头
Stone Plough
长 9.13 厘米　宽 7.42 厘米　厚 0.74 厘米
T0907 ⑤ e2: 7

石破土器
Stone Farm Tool
长 23.8 厘米　宽 15.9 厘米　厚 1.52 厘米
H65: 1

Chapter 1
篇章一 越海而来，文明肇始

石 管
Stone Tubular Bead
长 1.22 厘米　直径 0.94 厘米
M1∶1

石 管
Stone Tubular Bead
长 1.42 厘米　直径 0.99 厘米
M1∶4

石 环
Stone Ring
高 2 厘米　厚 1.3 厘米
T0807 ⑤ b1∶2

079

The Dawn of the Island | 海岛之光
大榭遗址出土文物精品图录

石纺轮
Stone Spinning Wheel
直径 3.4 厘米　厚 0.9 厘米
T0807 ⑤ c1：9

石纺轮
Stone Spinning Wheel
直径 3.2 厘米　厚 1 厘米
T0807 ⑤ c1：11

石纺轮
Stone Spinning Wheel
直径 3.8 厘米　厚 0.9 厘米
T0807 ⑤ c1：14

Chapter 1
篇章一 越海而来，文明肇始

石纺轮
Stone Spinning Wheel
直径 3.4 厘米　厚 1.1 厘米
T0906 ⑤ c1∶3

石纺轮
Stone Spinning Wheel
直径 3.6 厘米　厚 0.3 厘米
T1206 ⑤ c∶1

| The Dawn of the Island | 海 岛 之 光
大榭遗址出土文物精品图录

陶纺轮
Pottery Spinning Wheel
直径 3.2 厘米　厚 1 厘米
T0809 ⑤ a2：1

陶纺轮
Pottery Spinning Wheel
直径 3.8 厘米　厚 1.1 厘米
T1010 ⑤ a：3

陶纺轮
Pottery Spinning Wheel
直径 3.6 厘米　厚 1 厘米
T1205 ⑤ b：2

Chapter 1
篇章一　越海而来，文明肇始

陶纺轮
Pottery Spinning Wheel
直径 3.6 厘米　厚 1.3 厘米
T1208 ⑤ a:2

陶纺轮
Pottery Spinning Wheel
直径 5.2 厘米　厚 1.6 厘米
T1306 ⑤ b2:1

陶纺轮
Pottery Spinning Wheel
直径 3.2 厘米　厚 1.4 厘米
T1308 ⑤ a:3

The Dawn of the Island | 海岛之光
大榭遗址出土文物精品图录

砺 石
Grindstone
长 30.2 厘米　宽 10.2 厘米　厚 7.9 厘米
H28：1

Chapter 1
篇章一 越海而来，文明肇始

砺 石
Grindstone
长 15 厘米　宽 5.2 厘米　厚 4.5 厘米
T0807⑤f1:5

砺 石
Grindstone
长 17 厘米　宽 7 厘米　厚 5.4 厘米
T1407⑤a:3

The Dawn of the Island | 海 岛 之 光
大榭遗址出土文物精品图录

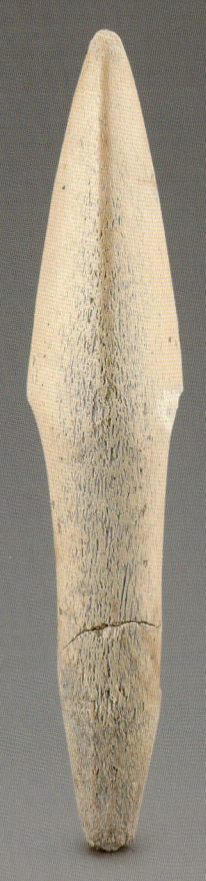

骨 镞
Bone Arrowhead
长 7.5 厘米
T0711 ⑤ c : 1

鹿 角
Deer Antler
T1207 ⑤ a : 5

Chapter 1
篇章一 越海而来，文明肇始

鹿 角
Deer Antler
T0806 ⑤ c1：33

The Dawn of the Island | 海岛之光
大榭遗址出土文物精品图录

鹿类下颌骨
Deer Mandible
T1010 ⑤ a: 19

猪下颌骨
Pig Mandible
长 30.5 厘米
T0910 ⑤ b: 7

Chapter 1
篇章一 越海而来，文明肇始

植物果核
Seeds
H25 ②: 6

葫芦籽
Gourd Seeds
H25 ②: 7

The Dawn of the Island | 海 岛 之 光
大榭遗址出土文物精品图录

大榭遗址二期遗存出土遗物
The Artefacts Unearthed from Daxie Site Phase 2

大榭遗址二期遗存出土遗物主要有较多陶器和少量石器，以及陆地、海洋动物骨骼。陶器群可分为日用器和制盐器两种：日用陶器较少，多为夹砂红褐陶和泥质灰陶，可辨器型见有鼎、豆、罐、盆、盘等，其既有比较典型的钱山漾文化特征，又有新的文化因素。制盐陶器数量较多，其中陶盐缸均为夹砂质地，大口、下腹斜收、圜底；陶盐盆则有夹植物和贝壳碎屑两种，均为大敞口、浅斜腹、大平底，器胎较厚，火候低。石器出土数量较少，可辨器型见有斧、锛、镞、刀等。玉器仅发现1件锥形器。动物骨骼主要为泥蚶，还有少量鹿类和猪骨骼。

The artefacts unearthed from Daxie Site Phase 2 include large amount of pottery wares and small amount of stone tools, as well as some terrestrial and marine fauna bones. Potteries found on site can be divided into daily wares and salt manufacture tools. The daily wares are found in small quantity, with majority of sandy clay reddish brown pottery and clay grey pottery, whose types contain tripod, stem dish, pot, basin, plate and so on. These wares not only bear typical features of Qianshanyang Culture but also integrated with new culture elements. On the other hand, salt manufacture tools are superior in numbers. The pottery jars for salt-making were made in sandy clay, with a large mouth, infundibular body and a spherical bottom. In addition, the pottery basins for salt-making were made in clay with plants debris as one kind and clay with shell debris as another. The basins were shaped in large open mouth, infundibular body with a small angle and a flat bottom, the body of which is relatively thick and fired with a low temperature. The stone tools were discovered in small amount, with identifiable types as axe, adze, arrowhead, knife and etc. Only one piece of cone-shaped tool made of jade has been found. The fauna remains were mostly clams as well as few deer and pig bones.

Chapter 1

篇章一　越海而来，文明肇始

陶盐缸
Pottery Salt-making Jar
高 28.6 厘米　口径 37.5 厘米
T0707 ④ g1 : 1

The Dawn of the Island | 海岛之光
大榭遗址出土文物精品图录

陶盐盆
Pottery Salt-making Basin
高 17.7 厘米 口径 46.3 厘米 底径 38.7 厘米
T0706 ④ b2: 2

陶盐盆
Pottery Salt-making Basin
高 13.8 厘米 口径 49.7 厘米 底径 40.5 厘米
TG10 ⑧: 7

Chapter 1
篇章一 越海而来，文明肇始

陶制盐支脚
Pottery Salt-making Stand
长 18.3 厘米　直径 6 厘米
TG5ST1B：2

陶制盐垫具
Pottery Salt-making Pad
长 16 厘米　宽 7.2 厘米　厚 9.2 厘米
T0712④d：1

The Dawn of the Island | 海 岛 之 光
大榭遗址出土文物精品图录

陶制盐垫具
Pottery Salt-making Pad
长 13.5 厘米　宽 8.7 厘米　厚 5.4 厘米
YZ22：1

陶盐盆内底面标本
Inner Surface of Pottery Salt-making Basin Sample
T0706 ④ a2：2

陶盐盆外底面标本
Outer Surface of Pottery Salt-making Basin Sample
T0807 ④ c：1

Chapter 1
篇章一 越海而来，文明肇始

陶 鼎
Pottery Tripod
高 29.3 厘米　口径 28.1 厘米　腹径 28.5 厘米
TG11⑧：1

陶 鼎
Pottery Tripod
高 23.4 厘米　口径 22.8 厘米　腹径 23.4 厘米
T0707 ④ g1 : 2

Chapter 1
篇章一 越海而来，文明肇始

陶 豆
Pottery Stem Dish
高 9.1 厘米　口径 21.8 厘米　底径 14.6 厘米
T0709 ④ g：9

The Dawn of the Island | 海岛之光
大榭遗址出土文物精品图录

陶 豆
Pottery Stem Dish
高 10.5 厘米　口径 19 厘米　底径 17.5 厘米
T0711 ④ g2 : 1

陶豆盘
Pottery Stem Plate
高 6.5 厘米　口径 23.4 厘米
TG8 ⑧ c : 1

Chapter 1
篇章一 越海而来，文明肇始

陶三足罐
Pottery Tripod Pot
高 25.6 厘米　口径 10.4 厘米
T0709 ④ g：10

The Dawn of | 海 岛 之 光
the Island | 大榭遗址出土文物精品图录

陶 杯
Pottery Cup

高 10 厘米　口径 6.6 厘米　底径 6.3 厘米
T0711 ④ g2: 2

陶器盖
Pottery Lid

高 8.6 厘米　底径 24.6 厘米
T0712 ④ f2: 1

Chapter 1
篇章一 越海而来，文明肇始

石 斧
Stone Axe
长 14.6 厘米　宽 6.2 厘米　厚 5.8 厘米
TG7 ①：1

有段石锛
Stone Stepped Adze
长 12.3 厘米　宽 6.13 厘米　厚 2.36 厘米
T0708 ④ d：1

The Dawn of | 海 岛 之 光
the Island | 大榭遗址出土文物精品图录

有段石锛
Stone Stepped Adze
长 11.1 厘米　宽 5.6 厘米　厚 1.2 厘米
TG7 ⑪ : 1

有段石锛
Stone Stepped Adze
长 9 厘米　宽 4.4 厘米　厚 2 厘米
T0809 ④ g : 1

Chapter 1

篇章一 越海而来，文明肇始

石锛半成品
Semi-finished Stone Adze
长 11.6 厘米　宽 4.2 厘米　厚 2.8 厘米
TG7ST5：2

石　锛
Stone Adze
长 9.5 厘米　宽 5.1 厘米　厚 2.2 厘米
T0608 ④ d：1

The Dawn of the Island | 海岛之光
大榭遗址出土文物精品图录

石 锛
Stone Adze
长 9 厘米　宽 5.5 厘米　厚 1.9 厘米
T0715 ④ f：1

弧刃石锛
Stone Adze with a Curved Blade
长 8.8 厘米　宽 4.6 厘米　厚 2.5 厘米
T0709 ④ g：8

石 刀
Stone Knife
长 8.8 厘米　宽 5.4 厘米　厚 1 厘米
T0814 ④ c：2

Chapter 1
篇章一　越海而来，文明肇始

石　镞
Stone Arrowhead
长 5.8 厘米　宽 2 厘米　厚 0.4 厘米
TG7ST5：3

石　镞
Stone Arrowhead
长 7.3 厘米　宽 2.2 厘米
T0709 ④ g：2

The Dawn of the Island | 海 岛 之 光
大榭遗址出土文物精品图录

石 镞
Stone Arrowhead
长 9 厘米
T0709 ④ g: 1

石 镞
Stone Arrowhead
长 7.5 厘米　宽 1.8 厘米　厚 0.8 厘米
T0709 ④ g: 7

Chapter 1

篇章一 越海而来,文明肇始

石 镞
Stone Arrowhead
长 7.7 厘米
T0808 ④ d2:3

石 镞
Stone Arrowhead
长 6.5 厘米　宽 1.8 厘米　厚 0.5 厘米
T0810 ④ f:1

The Dawn of the Island | 海岛之光
大榭遗址出土文物精品图录

石 镞
Stone Arrowhead
长 7.05 厘米　宽 1.9 厘米　厚 1.15 厘米
TG5④：1

石 镞
Stone Arrowhead
长 6.4 厘米　宽 1.6 厘米　厚 0.6 厘米
T0914④a：1

Chapter 1
篇章一 越海而来，文明肇始

石 镞
Stone Arrowhead
长 6.4 厘米　宽 2.8 厘米　厚 0.4 厘米
TG6 ⑦ c: 1

石 镞
Stone Arrowhead
长 7.1 厘米　宽 2.2 厘米
T1109 ④ b: 1

109

The Dawn of the Island | 海岛之光
大榭遗址出土文物精品图录

石 镞
Stone Arrowhead
长 7.2 厘米　宽 2.4 厘米　厚 0.4 厘米
TG5ST1B：1

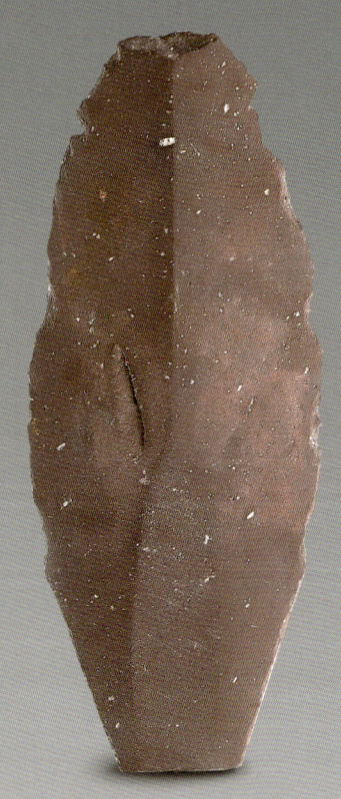

石 镞
Stone Arrowhead
长 6.5 厘米　宽 2.6 厘米　厚 0.4 厘米
TG8 ⑧ b：1

Chapter 1
篇章一 越海而来，文明肇始

石 镞
Stone Arrowhead
长 10.3 厘米 宽 1.8 厘米 厚 0.8 厘米
T0814 ④ c：1

石 镞
Stone Arrowhead
长 9.5 厘米 宽 2 厘米 厚 0.5 厘米
TG8 ⑧ b：2

The Dawn of the Island | 海 岛 之 光
大榭遗址出土文物精品图录

石　镞
Stone Arrowhead
长 4.6 厘米　宽 2.8 厘米　厚 0.3 厘米
TG6 ⑦ c：2

石　镞
Stone Arrowhead
长 4.8 厘米　宽 2 厘米　厚 0.2 厘米
TG7 ⑬ e：1

Chapter 1
篇章一 越海而来，文明肇始

石 球
Stone Ball
高 6.1 厘米
T1011 ④ a: 1

砺 石
Grindstone
长 19.2 厘米　宽 6.8 厘米　厚 6 厘米
T0808 ④ d2: 1

The Dawn of the Island | 海岛之光
大榭遗址出土文物精品图录

玉锥形器
Cone-shaped Jade
长 9.8 厘米　宽 1.1 厘米
T0809 ④ g：2

篇章二 Chapter 2

向海而生，
拓岛有成
——大榭遗址出土东周时期遗物

Island Exploitation
——Artefacts Excavated at Daxie Site in the Eastern Zhou Dynasty

当历史的车轮驶入东周时期，地处古代越国统辖范围内的大榭岛开始步入广域开发阶段。这一时期大榭岛上的海盐业，因为越国经济社会发展的需要而更趋兴盛，生产规模较之以前明显扩大，已经成为当时重要的经济支撑。当时先民的足迹几乎遍及大榭全岛，并在岛内各地留下了深深的时代印记。

由于保存不佳，考古发掘时在大榭遗址中仅发现了东周时期的蓄水坑、灰坑、灰沟、柱洞、木桩等遗迹10余处，但出土有陶、瓷、石、铜器等生产工具和生活用具50余件，以及少量动、植物遗存。其中质地坚硬的印纹硬陶、釉色莹润的原始瓷器和技艺精湛的青铜工具的发现，表明当时的大榭先民在生活水平与生产效率上已经有了质的飞跃。

在大榭岛的其他地方，还发现有多处东周时期的盐业生产遗存，显示这里自史前时期以来形成的盐业生产传统在继续发扬光大，且生产规模和产量有了显著提升，海岛开发进入了新的阶段。

Chapter 2

篇章二 向海而生，拓岛有成

When the wheel of history rolled into the Eastern Zhou Dynasty, Daxie Island, which was under the jurisdiction of the ancient Yue State, began to step in the stage of wide-area development. The salt production during this period had become more prosperous because of the needs of national economic and social development of the Yue State. The scale of production had expanded significantly, which became an important economic support then. The ancestors stepped almost the whole island, and deeply printed the mark of the era in different places on the island.

Due to poor preservation, only more than 10 archaeological features including storage pits, pits, ditches, post holes and posts of the Eastern Zhou Dynasty were found in Daxie Site during the archaeological excavation. However, there are more than 50 pieces of daily necessities and tools made of pottery, porcelain, stone, copper and so on, as well as a small number of animal and plant remains were excavated. The discovery of stamped hard pottery wares, lustrous glazed proto-porcelain wares and exquisite bronze tools indicated that during that time Daxie settlers had made a qualitative leap in living standards and production efficiency.

There are several salt production sites that origins from the Eastern Zhou Period distributed in other locations on Daxie Island. It indicates that the salt production formed in the prehistoric period was carried forward and further developed, with remarkably increasing scale and output. The exploitation of Daxie Island came into a new stage.

The Dawn of the Island | 海岛之光
大榭遗址出土文物精品图录

印纹硬陶鼎
Stamped Hard Pottery Tripod
高 29 厘米　口径 36.9 厘米　腹径 27.6 厘米
H85：2

Chapter 2
篇章二 向海而生，拓岛有成

印纹硬陶坛
Stamped Hard Pottery Jar
高 49.5 厘米　口径 19.8 厘米　腹径 40.5 厘米　底径 18.1 厘米
H2：1

The Dawn of the Island | 海岛之光
大榭遗址出土文物精品图录

陶 盆
Pottery Basin
高 6.9 厘米　口径 24.6 厘米　底径 15.6 厘米
T1010 ③ b：1

陶 盆
Pottery Basin
高 7.4 厘米　口径 24.4 厘米　底径 18 厘米
T1010 ③ b：2

Chapter 2
篇章二 向海而生，拓岛有成

侧视图
Side View

俯视图
Top View

原始瓷豆
Proto-porcelain Stem Dish
高 3.8 厘米　口径 11.2 厘米　底径 6 厘米
H1∶2

The Dawn of the Island | 海 岛 之 光
大榭遗址出土文物精品图录

原始瓷钵
Proto-porcelain Mortar
高 7.5 厘米　口径 15.7 厘米　底径 7.3 厘米
H1：3

原始瓷碗
Proto-porcelain Bowl
高 5 厘米　口径 14.2 厘米　底径 6.7 厘米
H2：2

Chapter 2
篇章二　向海而生，拓岛有成

原始瓷碗
Proto-porcelain Bowl
高 4.8 厘米　口径 14.5 厘米　底径 6 厘米
TG10 ②：4

原始瓷碗
Proto-porcelain Bowl
高 6.8 厘米　口径 11.2 厘米　底径 8.4 厘米
T0909 ①：2

123

The Dawn of the Island | 海 岛 之 光
大榭遗址出土文物精品图录

原始瓷杯
Proto-porcelain Cup
高 7 厘米　口径 5.4 厘米　底径 3.8 厘米
TG5 ①: 5

Chapter 2
篇章二 向海而生，拓岛有成

原始瓷杯
Proto-porcelain Cup
高 3.8 厘米　口径 5 厘米　底径 3.2 厘米
T0912②b：83

原始瓷杯
Proto-porcelain Cup
高 3.8 厘米　口径 5 厘米　底径 3.3 厘米
TG10②：1

The Dawn of the Island | 海岛之光
大榭遗址出土文物精品图录

原始瓷杯
Proto-porcelain Cup
高 5 厘米　口径 6.7 厘米　底径 4.8 厘米
TG5 ③：1

原始瓷杯
Proto-porcelain Cup
高 7.4 厘米　口径 8.6 厘米　底径 4.6 厘米
TG10 ②：3

Chapter 2

篇章二 向海而生，拓岛有成

石 镞
Stone Arrowhead
长 4.8 厘米　宽 2.2 厘米
T0710 ③：1

砺 石
Grindstone
长 7.3 厘米　宽 3 厘米　厚 2.5 厘米
H2：3

铜 耨
Bronze Hoe
长 14 厘米 宽 1 厘米
H1∶1

篇章三 Chapter 3

依海而兴，
丝路存迹

——大榭遗址出土宋元时期遗物

Maritime Silk Road Remains

——Artefacts Excavated at Daxie Site in Song Dynasty and Yuan Dynasty

海岛之光 | 大榭遗址出土文物精品图录
The Dawn of the Island

进入晚唐五代，特别是宋元时期，随着"海上丝绸之路"的繁荣发展与南北航路的纷纷开辟，明州（庆元）港跃升为当时中国乃至世界上最为知名的对外交通贸易口岸之一。

这一时期的大榭岛，因地处明州（庆元）港海道要冲而日益受到关注，海外交往一度十分频密。北宋《宣和奉使高丽图经》记载徐兢出使高丽时，曾途经"大小二谢山"[①]，大榭岛因作为当时"海上丝绸之路"的途经一站而得以永存史册。

在大榭遗址中发现了这一时期的柱洞、道路、灰坑、石砌护坡、排水设施等遗迹10余处，出土了大量陶质砖、瓦等建筑构件和碗、钵、碟、盏、罐、瓶、器盖等各色瓷器，以及石器、铜钱、铜镜等500余件。其中部分建筑构件档次高，暗示使用者拥有较高的身份和地位。瓷器以产自越窑、龙泉窑、湖田窑、吉州窑等当时国内诸多著名窑口者为主，其种类丰富、造型优美、釉色莹润，不排除在此中转外销的可能。

[①] 《宣和奉使高丽图经》卷三十四《海道一》"虎头山"条："其日申末刻，远望大小二谢山，历松柏湾，抵芦浦，抛矴，八舟同泊。"（北宋）徐兢撰：《宣和奉使高丽图经》，收入《丛书集成初编》第三二三六册，商务印书馆，1939年，第119页。

Chapter 3

篇章三 依海而兴，丝路存迹

Entering the late Tang Dynasty and the Five Dynasties, especially in the Song Dynasty and Yuan Dynasty, with the prosperity of the "Maritime Silk Road" and the opening up of the north and south routes, the Mingzhou (Qingyuan) port became one of the most famous foreign transportation and trade ports in China and even in the world at that time.

During this period, Daxie Island had received increasing attention due to its location as a key node on the routes of Mingzhou (Qingyuan) port, and the foreign exchanges had once flourished. *The Illustration of the Diplomatic Mission to Goryeo under the Emperor's Order in Xuanhe Period* in the Northern Song Dynasty, recorded that during Xu Jing's envoy to Goryeo, he passed through the "Daxie Mountain and Xiaoxie Mountain"[①]. As a stop in the "Maritime Silk Road", Daxie Island was recorded in the historical documentations.

More than 10 archaeological features of this period were found, including post holes, roads, pits, stone revetments and drainage facilities. The site also unearthed a large number of ceramic bricks, tiles and other building components, porcelain wares such as bowls, mortars, plates, small bowls, pots, bottles, lids, etc., as well as more than 500 pieces of stone tools, coins, bronze mirrors and so on. Part of the building components are elegant of high-grade, indicating the superior identity and social status of the users. In addition, the unearthed porcelains were produced from various well-known kilns in China at that time, such as Yue kiln, Longquan kiln, Hutian kiln and Jizhou kiln, which are rich in variety, appealing in designs, and shinning in glaze. There is a possibility that the porcelain wares were exported through the island.

---

① *Sea Route I*. From *the Illustration of the Diplomatic Mission to Goryeo under the Emperor's Order in Xuanhe Period*. Vol. 34. In the article of "Hutou Moutain": "At about five o' clock that afternoon, the Daxie Mountain and Xiaoxie Mountain were in the view from distance. After passing through Songbai Bay, we arrived and anchored off Lupu, where eight ships were berthed at the same time." Xujing. The Northern Song Dynasty. *The Illustration of the Diplomatic Mission to Goryeo under the Emperor's Order in Xuanhe Period*. 1939. From *The First Series of Complete Collection of Book*. No. 3236. Commercial Press, p119.

The Dawn of the Island | 海岛之光
大榭遗址出土文物精品图录

青白瓷三足炉
Bluish White Porcelain Tripod Censer
高 20.1 厘米　口径 18.3 厘米　足高 5.9 厘米
T0912 ② b：1

Chapter 3

篇章三 依海而兴，丝路存迹

青白瓷盖罐
Bluish White Porcelain Pot with Lid
高 6 厘米　口径 4.6 厘米　底径 4.6 厘米
T0610 ①: 3

The Dawn of the Island | 海岛之光
大榭遗址出土文物精品图录

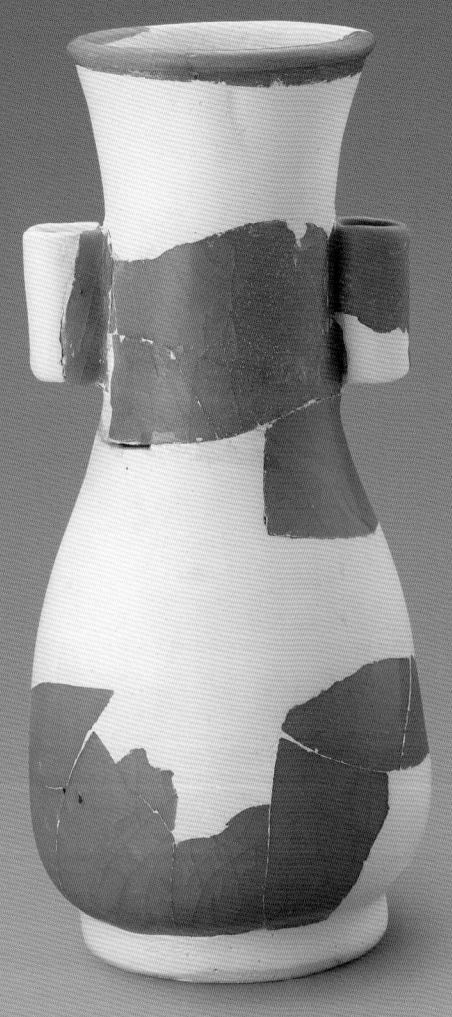
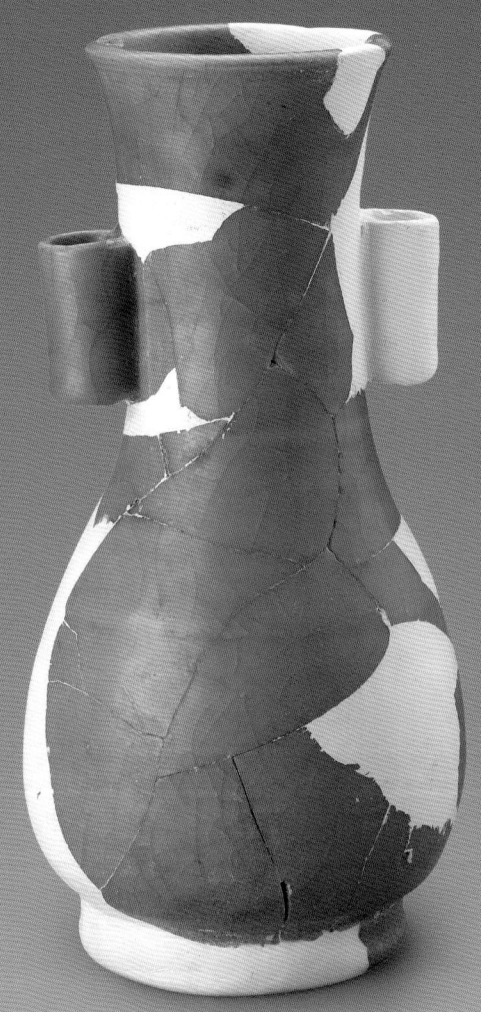

青瓷贯耳瓶（一对）
A Pair of Celadon Vases with Double Ears
高 26.7 厘米　口径 9 厘米　底径 9 厘米
高 26.7 厘米　口径 8.8 厘米　底径 9.2 厘米
T0709 ②∶8

Chapter 3

篇章三 依海而兴,丝路存迹

青白瓷执壶
Bluish White Porcelain Ewer
残高 19.3 厘米　口径 10.5 厘米
T0912 ② b：34

青瓷水注
Celadon Water Dropper
高 7.2 厘米　口径 2.9 厘米　底径 6 厘米
T1012 ② b：1

Chapter 3

篇章三 依海而兴，丝路存迹

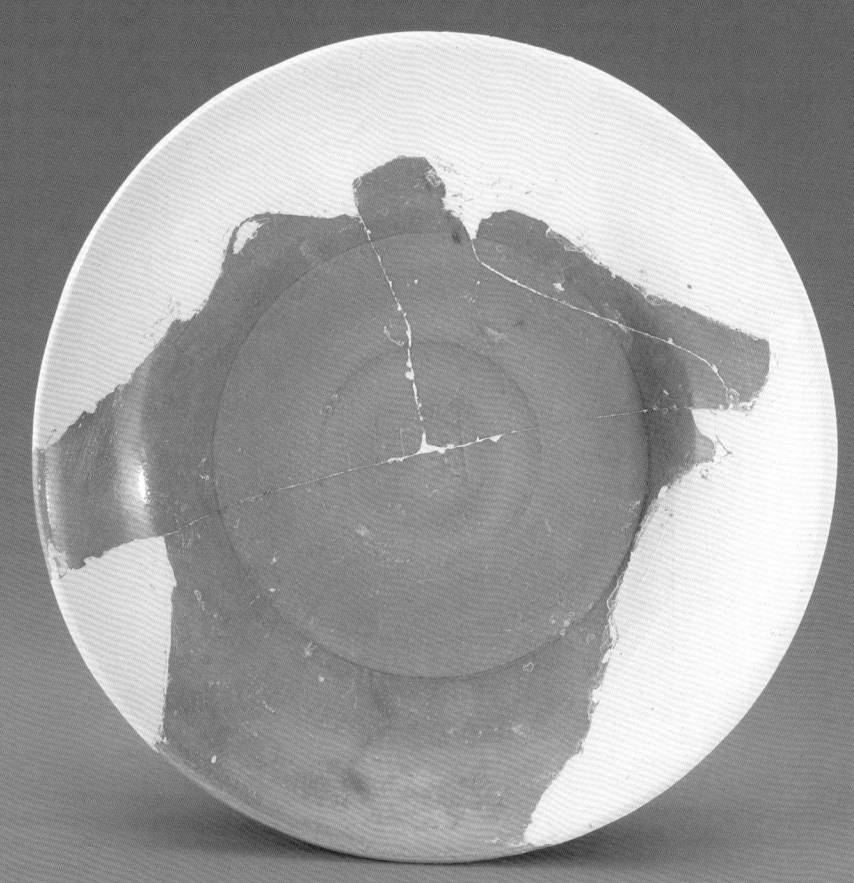

顶视图
Vertical View

侧视图
Side View

"金玉满堂"款识青瓷盘
Celadon Plate with Inscription "Jinyumantang"
高 3.4 厘米　口径 14.9 厘米　底径 5.4 厘米
T0912 ② b：26

The Dawn of the Island | 海岛之光
大榭遗址出土文物精品图录

"东嘉遗范"款识青瓷碗
Celadon Bowl with Inscription "Dongjiayifan"
残高 5.4 厘米　底径 6 厘米
T1011 ② b：70

Chapter 3
篇章三 依海而兴，丝路存迹

顶视图
Vertical View

侧视图
Side View

青瓷双鱼洗
Celadon Washer with Double Fish Pattern
高 4 厘米　口径 13 厘米　底径 6.1 厘米
T0911 ② b：44

The Dawn of | 海岛之光
the Island | 大榭遗址出土文物精品图录

顶视图
Vertical View

侧视图
Side View

青瓷双鱼洗
Celadon Washer with Double Fish Pattern
高 6.4 厘米　口径 22.9 厘米　底径 12.3 厘米
T1011 ② b：40

Chapter 3

篇章三 依海而兴，丝路存迹

青瓷折沿洗
Celadon Washer with Folded Rim
高 5.3 厘米　口径 22 厘米　底径 10.4 厘米
T1012 ② b: 20

The Dawn of | 海 岛 之 光
the Island | 大榭遗址出土文物精品图录

青瓷折沿盘
Celadon Plate with Folded Rim
高 7.4 厘米　口径 20.9 厘米　底径 13.2 厘米
H86：2

Chapter 3
篇章三 依海而兴，丝路存迹

青瓷折沿盘
Celadon Plate with Folded Rim
高 3.9 厘米 口径 12.8 厘米 底径 5.9 厘米
T1011 ② b: 56

青瓷莲瓣纹盘
Celadon Plate with Lotus-petal Pattern
高 4.4 厘米 口径 16 厘米 底径 6 厘米
T0912 ② b: 6

The Dawn of the Island | 海岛之光
大榭遗址出土文物精品图录

顶视图
Vertical View

侧视图
Side View

青瓷莲瓣纹盘
Celadon Plate with Lotus-petal Pattern
高 5 厘米　口径 17.9 厘米　底径 8 厘米
T1011 ② b：48

Chapter 3
篇章三 依海而兴，丝路存迹

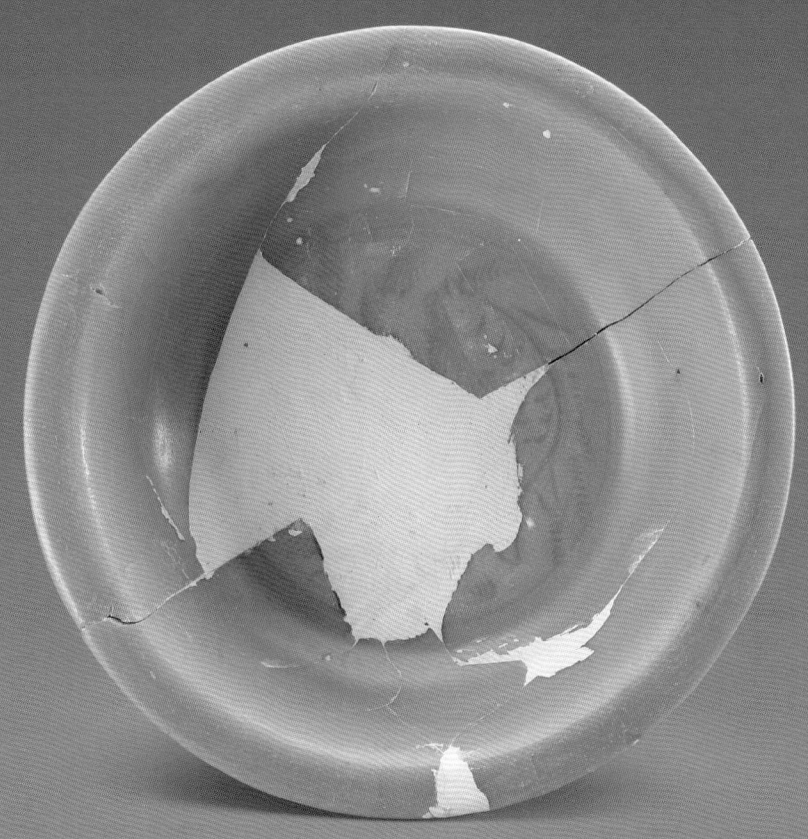

顶视图
Vertical View

侧视图
Side View

青瓷莲瓣纹盘
Celadon Plate with Lotus-petal Pattern
高 4.5 厘米　口径 16.5 厘米　底径 7.9 厘米
T0912②b：3

The Dawn of the Island | **海 岛 之 光**
大榭遗址出土文物精品图录

顶视图
Vertical View

侧视图
Side View

青瓷莲瓣纹盘
Celadon Plate with Lotus-petal Pattern
高 4.8 厘米　口径 16.5 厘米　底径 8.3 厘米
T1011 ② b：64

Chapter 3

篇章三 依海而兴,丝路存迹

底视图
Bottom View

侧视图
Side View

青瓷莲瓣纹盘
Celadon Plate with Lotus-petal Pattern
高 4.4 厘米　口径 15.8 厘米　底径 6 厘米
T0911 ② b: 124

The Dawn of | 海 岛 之 光
the Island | 大榭遗址出土文物精品图录

青白瓷芒口碗
Bluish White Porcelain Bowl with Unglazed Rim
高 7.5 厘米　口径 17.9 厘米　底径 5.7 厘米
T0911 ② b：103

青白瓷芒口碗
Bluish White Porcelain Bowl with Unglazed Rim
高 8.7 厘米　口径 19.8 厘米　底径 6.2 厘米
T0911 ② b：90

青白瓷芒口碗
Bluish White Porcelain Bowl with Unglazed Rim
高 7.1 厘米　口径 12.9 厘米　底径 5.2 厘米
T1012②b：7

青白瓷芒口碗
Bluish White Porcelain Bowl with Unglazed Rim
高 7.1 厘米　口径 16.4 厘米　底径 5.4 厘米
T0912②b：30

青白瓷芒口碗
Bluish White Porcelain Bowl with Unglazed Rim
高 7.8 厘米   口径 15.7 厘米   底径 5.2 厘米
T1012 ② b: 22

Chapter 3

篇章三 依海而兴,丝路存迹

顶视图
Vertical View

侧视图
Side View

青白瓷芒口碗
Bluish White Porcelain Bowl with Unglazed Rim
高 4.6 厘米　口径 17.7 厘米　底径 6.1 厘米
T0911 ② b: 28

青白瓷碗
Bluish White Porcelain Bowl
高 6 厘米　口径 16.5 厘米　底径 5.5 厘米
T1011 ② b：12

青白瓷碗
Bluish White Porcelain Bowl
高 7.3 厘米　口径 16.1 厘米　底径 5.5 厘米
T0912 ② b：7

Chapter 3
篇章三　依海而兴，丝路存迹

顶视图
Vertical View

侧视图
Side View

青白瓷芒口洗
Bluish White Porcelain Washer with Unglazed Rim
高 2.8 厘米　口径 13.8 厘米　底径 9.4 厘米
T0911 ② b: 29

青白瓷芒口洗
Bluish White Porcelain Washer with Unglazed Rim
高 2.8 厘米　口径 10.1 厘米　底径 5.5 厘米
T1012 ② b：2

Chapter 3

篇章三 依海而兴，丝路存迹

顶视图
Vertical View

侧视图
Side View

青瓷碗
Celadon Bowl
高 7.2 厘米　口径 16.6 厘米　底径 6.5 厘米
T0911 ② b: 97

The Dawn of the Island | 海 岛 之 光
大榭遗址出土文物精品图录

顶视图
Vertical View

侧视图
Side View

青瓷碗
Celadon Bowl
高 7.5 厘米　口径 17.1 厘米　底径 6.3 厘米
T0912 ② b: 21

Chapter 3

篇章三 依海而兴,丝路存迹

顶视图
Vertical View

侧视图
Side View

青瓷碗
Celadon Bowl
高 7 厘米 口径 16.4 厘米 底径 6.4 厘米
T0911 ② b: 92

The Dawn of the Island | 海岛之光
大榭遗址出土文物精品图录

顶视图
Vertical View

侧视图
Side View

青瓷莲瓣纹碗
Celadon Bowl with Lotus-petal Pattern
高 6.7 厘米　口径 17.1 厘米　底径 5.7 厘米
T1011 ② b: 37

Chapter 3
篇章三 依海而兴，丝路存迹

青瓷莲瓣纹碗
Celadon Bowl with Lotus-petal Pattern
高 9.4 厘米　口径 20.8 厘米　底径 6.9 厘米
T0911②b:14

底视图
Bottom View

侧视图
Side View

青瓷莲瓣纹碗
Celadon Bowl with Lotus-petal Pattern
高 6.5 厘米　口径 15.6 厘米　底径 5.3 厘米
T0911 ② b: 17

Chapter 3
篇章三 依海而兴，丝路存迹

青瓷莲瓣纹碗
Celadon Bowl with Lotus-petal Pattern
高 7.8 厘米　口径 12.8 厘米　底径 6.9 厘米
T0911 ② b：26

青瓷莲瓣纹碗
Celadon Bowl with Lotus-petal Pattern
高 6.3 厘米　口径 12.8 厘米　底径 3.4 厘米
T1012 ② b：15

青瓷莲瓣纹碗
Celadon Bowl with Lotus-petal Pattern
高 6.9 厘米　口径 16.2 厘米　底径 5.3 厘米
T0911 ② b：109

The Dawn of the Island | 海岛之光
大榭遗址出土文物精品图录

底视图
Bottom View

侧视图
Side View

青白瓷莲瓣纹芒口碗
Bluish White Porcelain Bowl with Lotus-petal Pattern and Unglazed Rim
高 4.3 厘米　口径 16.8 厘米　底径 5 厘米
T0911 ② b: 73

Chapter 3
篇章三 依海而兴,丝路存迹

黑瓷盏
Black Porcelain Small Bowl
高 4.1 厘米　口径 9.6 厘米　底径 3.2 厘米
T1011 ② b: 38

黑瓷盏
Black Porcelain Small Bowl
高 4.6 厘米　口径 10.1 厘米　底径 3.2 厘米
T1012 ② b: 6

黑瓷盏
Black Porcelain Small Bowl
高 5 厘米　口径 10.6 厘米　底径 3.7 厘米
T0912 ② b: 11

The Dawn of the Island | 海岛之光
大榭遗址出土文物精品图录

黑瓷剪纸纹盏
Black Porcelain Tea Bowl with Paper-cut Design
高 5.7 厘米
T0911 ② b：148

Chapter 3

篇章三 依海而兴，丝路存迹

褐釉三系罐
Brown Glazed Pot with Three Loop Lugs
高 21.3 厘米　口径 8.4 厘米　底径 7.8 厘米
T0705 ①：1

陶　壶
Pottery Jug
高 22 厘米　口径 10 厘米　底径 8 厘米
T0911 ② b：71

165

The Dawn of the Island | 海岛之光
大榭遗址出土文物精品图录

韩 瓶
Han Bottle
高 21.3 厘米　口径 7 厘米　底径 7.2 厘米
T0911 ② b: 8

韩 瓶
Han Bottle
高 19.8 厘米　口径 5.8 厘米　底径 6.2 厘米
T0911 ② b: 30

Chapter 3

篇章三 依海而兴,丝路存迹

韩 瓶
Han Bottle
高 24.5 厘米　口径 8.5 厘米　底径 7.5 厘米
T0911 ② b: 31

韩 瓶
Han Bottle
高 23.6 厘米　口径 7.3 厘米　底径 7.6 厘米
T0911 ② b: 34

The Dawn of | 海 岛 之 光
the Island | 大榭遗址出土文物精品图录

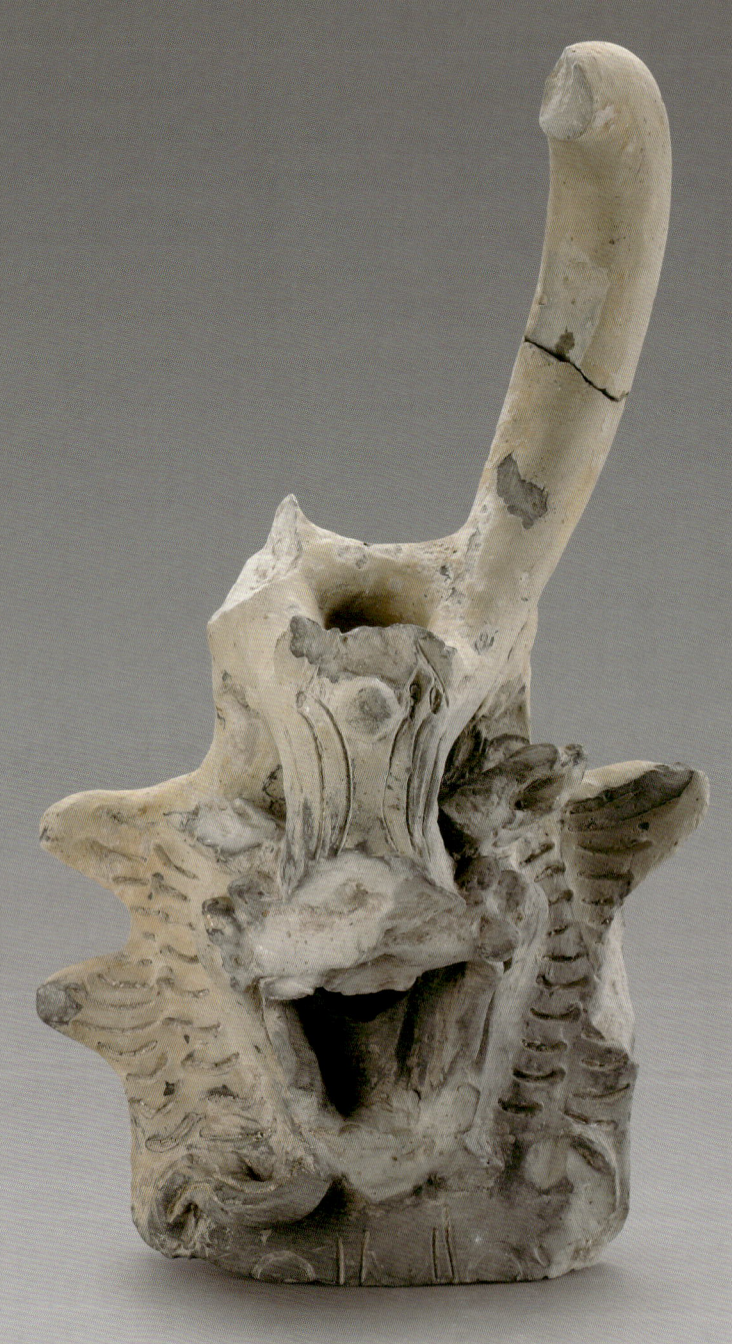

陶龙首形鸱吻
Pottery Ridge Beast with Dragon Head Design
残长 37.9 厘米　残宽 22.4 厘米　残高 12.6 厘米
T0912 ② b：70

Chapter 3
篇章三 依海而兴，丝路存迹

陶器座
Pottery Pedestal
残高 19 厘米　底径 27.5 厘米
T1011 ② b: 30

陶建筑构件
Pottery Building Component
长 13.4 厘米　高 7 厘米
T1011 ② b: 34

The Dawn of the Island | 海岛之光
大榭遗址出土文物精品图录

陶排水管
Pottery Drain Pipe
长 68 厘米 直径 24.2 厘米
T1010 ② c: 2

Chapter 3
篇章三 依海而兴，丝路存迹

瓦 当
Tile End
直径 13.1 厘米
T0911 ② b：106

瓦 当
Tile End
直径 15.8 厘米
T0911 ② c：3

The Dawn of the Island | 海岛之光
大榭遗址出土文物精品图录

瓦 当
Tile End
直径 13.1 厘米
T0912②b:89

瓦 当
Tile End
直径 13.6 厘米
T1011②a:1

Chapter 3
篇章三 依海而兴，丝路存迹

石 臼
Stone Mortar
高 12 厘米　口径 29.6 厘米　底径 19 厘米
T0912 ② b：22

石覆莲经幢座
Lotus Shaped Stone Sutra Pillar Foundation
高 27 厘米　底径 38 厘米
T0912 ② b：92

The Dawn of the Island | 海 岛 之 光
大榭遗址出土文物精品图录

石 球
Stone Ball
最长 5.2 厘米　最宽 4.2 厘米　最高 2.6 厘米
T0911 ② b：144-2

石 球
Stone Ball
最长 8.9 厘米　最宽 7.8 厘米　最高 5.6 厘米
T1011 ② b：39

Chapter 3
篇章三 依海而兴，丝路存迹

铜 镜
Bronze Mirror
长 13.7 厘米　镜面直径 8 厘米　柄长 5.8 厘米
T0609 ①：1

考古大事记

1980 年 9 月　　遗址所在地村民烧窑取土时，曾挖出一些新石器时代的磨制石器并上交国家保管，由此引起了文物部门的注意。

2008 年 6 月　　宁波市第三次全国文物普查时，正式确认了遗址的存在，当时定名为"东岳宫遗址"。

2010 年 10 月　　遗址入选"宁波市第三次全国文物普查百大新发现"之一。

2015 年 4 月至 5 月　　宁波市文物考古研究所组织专业人员对遗址进行多次地面踏查和随机勘探。

2015 年 9 月至 12 月　　宁波市文物考古研究所主持对遗址进行考古勘探和局部试掘。

2015 年 12 月 17 日　　"大榭东岳宫遗址考古试掘专家论证会"在大榭开发区管委会召开。根据专家意见，因"东岳宫遗址"名称易引发歧义，遂将其更名为"大榭遗址"。

2016 年 4 月至 12 月　　宁波市文物考古研究所主持对遗址实施 I 期考古发掘，发掘面积 4000 平方米。

2016 年 9 月 27 日　　"大榭遗址考古发掘第一次专家论证会"在国家水下文化遗产保护宁波基地召开。

2016 年 12 月　　遗址获评 2016 年度"浙江考古重要发现"。

2017 年 3 月至 12 月　　宁波市文物考古研究所主持对遗址实施 II 期考古发掘，发掘面积 3000 平方米。

2017 年 11 月 10 日　　"大榭遗址考古发掘第二次专家论证会"在大榭国际大酒店召开。

2017 年 12 月　　遗址获评 2017 年度"浙江考古重要发现"。

2018 年 1 月　　遗址入选 2017 年度"全国十大考古新发现"初评名单。

2018 年 2 月　　遗址入选 2017 年度"全国十大考古新发现"终评名单。

2018 年 3 月 10 日　　"浙江宁波大榭史前制盐遗址考古项目评估会"在国家水下文化遗产保护宁波基地召开。

2018 年 5 月　　"浙江宁波大榭史前制盐遗址考古发掘项目"获评 2017 年度"全国十大考古新发现"入围项目。

2018 年 10 月　　"浙江宁波大榭史前制盐遗址考古发掘项目"获评全国"田野考古奖"二等奖。

2019 年 9 月 17 日　　"海岛之光——大榭遗址考古成果展"完成布展工作。

CHRONICLES

In September 1980, when the villagers in the area where the site was located took soil for ceramic firing, some Neolithic stone tools were discovered and handed over to the state later. From then the place attracted the attention of the cultural relics department.

In June 2008, the Third National Survey of Cultural Heritage in Ningbo officially confirmed the existence of the site, which was then named as "Dongyuegong Site".

In October 2010, the site was selected as one of the "Top 100 New Discoveries in the Third National Survey of Cultural Heritage in Ningbo".

From April to May 2015, Ningbo Municipal Institute of Cultural Relics and Archaeology organized professionals to conduct multiple ground investigations and random surveys of the site.

From September to December 2015, Ningbo Municipal Institute of Cultural Relics and Archaeology hosted the archaeological survey and partial trial excavation of the site.

On December 17, 2015, "The Expert Seminar on Archaeological Trial Excavation of Dongyuegong Site in Daxie Island" was held in the Daxie Development Zone Administrative Committee. According to the opinions of the experts, as the name of "Dongyuegong Site" was likely to cause ambiguity, it was renamed as "Daxie Site".

From April to December 2016, Ningbo Municipal Institute of Cultural Relics and Archaeology conducted the first archaeological excavation on the site, with the excavation area of 4,000 square meters.

On September 27, 2016, "The First Expert Seminar on Archaeological Excavation of Daxie Site" was held at the Ningbo Base, National Center of Underwater Cultural Heritage.

In December 2016, the site was awarded "The Important Archaeological Discoveries of Zhejiang" in 2016.

From March to December 2017, Ningbo Municipal Institute of Cultural Relics and Archaeology conducted the second archaeological excavation on the site, with the excavation area of 3,000 square meters.

On November 10, 2017, "The Second Expert Seminar on Archaeological Excavation of Daxie Site" was held in Daxie International Hotel.

In December 2017, the site was awarded "The Important Archaeological Discoveries of Zhejiang" in 2017.

In January 2018, the site was selected on the preliminary review list of "The National Top Ten Archaeological New Discoveries" in 2017.

In February 2018, the site was selected on the final list of "The National Top Ten Archaeological New Discoveries" in 2017.

On March 10, 2018, "The Evaluation Meeting of the Archaeological Program of the Prehistoric Salt Manufacture Site in Daxie Island, Ningbo City, Zhejiang Province" was held at the Ningbo Base, National Center of Underwater Cultural Heritage.

In May 2018, "The Archaeological Excavation Program of the Prehistoric

Salt Manufacture Site in Daxie Island, Ningbo City, Zhejiang Province" was selected as the finalist of "The National Top Ten Archaeological New Discoveries" in 2017.

In October 2018, "The Archaeological Excavation Program of the Prehistoric Salt Manufacture Site in Daxie Island, Ningbo City, Zhejiang Province" won the second prize of "the National Field Archaeology Award".

On September 17, 2019, the preparation of "The Dawn of the Island—The Exhibition of Archaeological Achievements at Daxie Site" was finished.

后 记

作为中国古代海盐业制作的最早实证和大榭岛悠久历史的物质见证,大榭遗址的发现与发掘,不仅收获了诸多的行业殊荣,也引发了世人的广泛关注。在考古发掘简报和专题考古报告正式发表(出版)之前,我们编著这样一本精品文物图录,既有以雅俗共赏、直观易懂的形式来阐释、图说大榭遗址前世今生之意愿,也有感谢方方面面支持并回应社会各界诉求之考量,更希望能够借此更好地促进大榭遗址的保护与研究、宣传与展示。

本书由王结华主持策划并主编,雷少任执行主编,张华琴、梅术文任副主编。文稿由王结华、雷少、毕显忠、张华琴共同撰写;照片由胡冬青、刘翀摄制;文物由史吾平、姚宏均、李养科、郭宗录、王伟国、郑卫国修复;英文由周昳恒、洪欣翻译。全书最后由王结华、雷少负责修订、润色并统稿完成。

本书原定于2019年出版,因种种原因,特别是受疫情影响而拖延至今。值此书稿正式付梓之际,再次向为大榭遗址发掘、保护和本书编著、出版付出辛勤努力的所有同仁致以衷心谢忱!

由于编者水平有限,本书中出现的疏漏与错误在所难免,尚祈各位读者见谅并指正。

编 者

2021 年 3 月

AFTERWORD

The discovery and excavation of Daxie Site, which serves not only as the earliest evidence of salt production in ancient China, but also as the physical proof of the prolonged history of Daxie Island, has earned numerous honors in archaeology and drawn worldwide attentions. Before the official publication of the brief excavation report and special archaeological report of the site, we have compiled this book for artefacts collection. It is in an effort to explain and illustrate the aspirations of the past and present of Daxie Site in a visualized and comprehensible form, suiting both refined and popular tastes. This book also serves as the appreciation for the assistance from various sides, and a response to the appeals from all sectors of society. Over and above that, it is our sincere hope that our effort can promote the preservation, research, publicity and exhibition of Daxie Site.

The book is planned and edited by Wang Jiehua, with Lei Shao as executive editor, Zhang Huaqin and Mei Shuwen as deputy editors. The manuscript was jointly written by Wang Jiehua, Lei Shao, Bi Xianzhong and Zhang Huaqin; photos were provided by Hu Dongqing and Liu Chong; artefacts were restored by Shi Wuping, Yao Hongjun, Li Yangke, Guo Zonglu, Wang Weiguo and Zheng Weiguo; the book was translated by Zhou Yiheng and Hong Xin. Wang Jiehua was responsible for revising, polishing and unifying the whole manuscript.

The original plan for the publication of the book was in 2019. However, due to many problems, especially the coronavirus pandemic it has not

Afterword
后 记

been completed until today. We would like to take the opportunity of this publication to express again our sincere gratitude to the people who devoted to the excavation and protection of Daxie Site, as well as to whom pay their effort to the edition and publication of this book.

In view of the limited capacity of the compiler, there are inevitably omissions and errors in the book. I hereby appeal for your pardon and your corrections will be greatly appreciated.

Editor
March 2021

图书在版编目（CIP）数据

海岛之光：大榭遗址出土文物精品图录 / 宁波市文化遗产管理研究院，大榭开发区社会发展保障局，北仑区文物保护管理所编著． -- 宁波：宁波出版社，2021.5

ISBN 978-7-5526-4158-5

Ⅰ．①海⋯ Ⅱ．①宁⋯ ②大⋯ ③北⋯ Ⅲ．①文化遗址—出土文物—宁波—图集 Ⅳ．① K878.02

中国版本图书馆 CIP 数据核字（2020）第 246849 号

海岛之光：大榭遗址出土文物精品图录
The Dawn of the Island : The Essential Collection of Archaeological Artefacts at Daxie Site

宁波市文化遗产管理研究院
宁波大榭开发区社会发展保障局　编著
北 仑 区 文 物 保 护 管 理 所

出版发行	宁波出版社
地　　址	宁波市甬江大道1号宁波书城8号楼6楼
邮　　编	315040
联系电话	0574-87259609
网　　址	http://www.nbcbs.com
责任编辑	苗梁婕　陈凌欧
责任校对	虞姬颖
装帧设计	马　力
印　　刷	宁波白云印刷有限公司
开　　本	787毫米×1092毫米　1 / 16
印　　张	11.75
字　　数	200千
版　　次	2021年5月第1版
印　　次	2021年5月第1次印刷
标准书号	ISBN 978-7-5526-4158-5
定　　价	280.00元

本书若有倒装缺页影响阅读,请与出版社联系调换,电话：0574-87248279